C. Van Eaton
6445 Ridge Lake
Hixson, TN 37343

POLITICAL THEORY AND PUBLIC CHOICE

Political Theory and Public Choice

The Selected Essays of Anthony Downs Volume One

Anthony Downs

Senior Fellow, The Brookings Institution, USA

Edward Elgar

Cheltenham, UK • Northampton, MA, USA

Published by
Edward Elgar Publishing Limited
8 Lansdown Place
Cheltenham
Glos GL50 2HU
UK

Edward Elgar Publishing, Inc.
6 Market Street
Northampton
Massachusetts 01060
USA

A catalogue record for this book
is available from the British Library

Library of Congress Cataloguing in Publication Data

Downs, Anthony.
    Political theory and public choice / Anthony Downs.
        (The selected essays of Anthony Downs ; v. 1)
    1. Political science. 2. Social choice. I. Title. II. Series:
Downs, Anthony. Essays. Selections ; v. 1.
JA71.D68 1998
320'.01'1—dc21   98–12621
                                                                         CIP

ISBN 1 85898 733 4

Printed and bound in Great Britain by MPG Books Ltd, Bodmin, Cornwall

Contents

Acknowledgements

The views in this work are solely those of the author, and not necessarily those of the Brookings Institution, its Trustees, or its members of Staff.

The author and publishers wish to thank the following who have kindly given permission for the use of copyright material.

Dædalus for article: 'The Evolution of Democracy: How Its Axioms and Institutional Forms Have Been Adapted to Changing Social Forces', **116** (3), Summer 1987, 119–48.

Johns Hopkins University Press for article: 'Why the Government Budget is too Small in a Democracy', *World Politics*, **XII** (4), July 1960, 541–63.

New School for Social Research for article: 'The Public Interest: Its Meaning in a Democracy', *Social Research*, **XXIX** (1), Spring 1962, 1–36.

Public Interest for article: 'Up and Down with Ecology – the "Issue-Attention Cycle"', **28**, Summer 1972, 38–50.

Rand McNally for excerpt: 'Separating the Planning and Procurement of Public Services from their Production and Delivery' in *Urban Problems and Prospects*, 2nd edition, 1976, 227–42.

University of Chicago Press for articles: 'An Economic Theory of Political Action in a Democracy', *Journal of Political Economy*, **LXV** (2), April 1957, 135–50; 'In Defense of Majority Voting', *Journal of Political Economy*, **LXIX** (2), April 1961, 192–9; 'A Theory of Large Managerial Firms', with R. Joseph Monsen, Jr, *Journal of Political Economy*, **LXXIII** (3), June 1965, 221–36.

The Wall Street Journal for article: 'They Sell Sizzle, but Their Predictions Fizzle', Editorial Page, April 6, 1983.

Every effort has been made to trace all the copyright holders but if any have been inadvertently overlooked the publishers will be pleased to make the necessary arrangements at the first opportunity.

Introduction: Confessions of an economic theorist and urban policy analyst

When Edward Elgar, the publisher of this volume, asked me to write an introduction to my collected articles, he urged me to make it mainly autobiographical. Yet I also wanted to explain certain basic aspects of my approaches to the two fields in which I have written. This introduction seeks to satisfy both these objectives.

My professional writings concern two distinct and very different subject areas. One set of works consists of rather abstract analyses of the political theory of democracy. These include *An Economic Theory of Democracy* (1957), *Inside Bureaucracy* (1967) and about a dozen related articles. These writings are based largely upon extensive logical deductions from a few simple premises of economic thought. The other set of works contains a much larger number of more practically-oriented studies concerning real estate and urban affairs. These include 15 books ranging from *Opening Up the Suburbs* (1973) through *Neighborhoods and Urban Development* (1981) and *Stuck in Traffic* (1992) to *New Visions for Metropolitan America* (1994) and *A Reevaluation of Residential Rent Control* (1997) plus over three hundred articles. These works are based mainly upon empirical data and inductive reasoning from field observations, research carried out by others, and my own practical experience.

These two areas of concern differ not only in subject matter, but also in the basic manner in which each is approached. Both differences are rooted in the circumstances under which I initially entered these fields, and subsequently pursued them. Yet both share two basic goals: penetrating beneath surface phenomena by understanding the most fundamental forces involved, and explaining how those forces operate in simple language comprehensible to any reader.

My initial forays into professional writing concerned sports. In high school, I was hired by the local weekly newspaper in Park Ridge, Illinois, a suburb of Chicago where I grew up, to cover local summer softball leagues. This assignment expanded into high school football and other sports, and I soon became the sports editor of that paper. My sports writing career continued on the student newspaper at Carleton College, in Northfield, Minnesota, 40 miles south of Minneapolis. There I also expanded into play-by-play broadcasting of football and basketball games on our college radio station. This experience taught me to write in language simple enough so that even local softball aficionados would understand every nuance, but colourful enough to retain the readers' attention.

While in college, I began writing articles on real estate subjects, thanks to the nepotism of my father, James C. Downs Jr. He was the editor of a magazine for property managers imaginatively titled *The Journal of Property Management*. He needed articles to fill the magazine during months when good manuscripts from the profession failed to appear. So he started giving me writing assignments. One of my first assignments was to write about the then new trend towards much larger automobile service stations. I complained that no information would be available about such a specialized subject. To my astonishment, I discovered there were two monthly magazines published solely about retail gas stations, as well as a large professional society of gas station owners and operators which held many meetings and yearly conventions. I have since learned that almost every activity in America, no matter how narrowly defined or seemingly trivial, has a similarly active following with its own societies, publications, conventions, political interests, terminology and legends.

All the articles I wrote for my father were totally practical, based upon some solid empirical data plus many anecdotes, and written to inform people working in real estate daily. He insisted on simple language and an easily-comprehensible style, to which I often added the colourful verb forms typical of sports writing (teams do not just win, they 'edge', 'crush' or 'blast' their opponents).

At the same time, two aspects of college life were pushing me towards trying to discover the fundamental forces at work concerning each subject, rather than looking only superficially at current trends. The first was a demanding English professor who assigned short essays analysing specific aspects of famous poems and plays. The second was my experience as a lowly freshman on the college debating team. I was a practising Roman Catholic, but all the other debaters – mainly upperclassmen – were sceptical agnostics contemptuous of religion in general and Catholicism in particular. They verbally assaulted my religious beliefs at every opportunity. In self-defence, I taught myself much Catholic theology by reading St Thomas Aquinas and other saints and philosophers. This required me to penetrate beneath the surfaces of daily religious practices and views to core theology and historical arguments. Moreover, I had to defend these complex ideas in relatively simple language.

One other aspect of my college life proved even more crucial to my later professional writings: this was running for president of the student body during my junior year at Carleton. I wanted to win, but I had no specific policy goals in mind. So my friends and I had to invent a whole platform just to have something to talk about. We then vigorously advocated every plank in that platform as though it had been divinely revealed to us. After I won the election, I conscientiously tried to achieve each of my ten explicit campaign goals – and accomplished almost all of them in the subsequent year.

To my chagrin, no one paid the slightest attention to my brilliant achievements in office. Student apathy towards my administration was total. Naturally, I did not want to attribute this mass ennui to my own incompetence or boring personality. Rather, I justified this outcome by concluding that students were indifferent because the results of my policies did not really affect them much. In fact, most of my policy results involved details of campus life of which they were not aware. And they were too busy doing more interesting things to worry about their student government.

So I formulated the hypothesis that voters in this particular democracy were *rationally ignorant* about their government's affairs. It was not time-efficient for them to stay well-informed about the details of student government, or whether the people they elected actually kept their promises. Doing so would not affect their lives much, but would consume a great deal of time and effort more fruitfully spent on other activities. This insight, plus the idea that candidates for office are more interested in winning than in carrying out particular policies, were two foundations of my later work *An Economic Theory of Democracy*.

After graduating from Carleton, I went to Stanford University to obtain a doctorate in economics – a subject on which I had not had a single course before arriving there. I completed my course work in three years and set about selecting a topic for my Ph.D. thesis. My first choice proved impractical, even though I had won a Social Science Research Council scholarship to pursue it. So I began casting about for an alternative subject. Professor Julius Margolis suggested that I explore an idea from Joseph Schumpeter's classic, *Capitalism, Socialism, and Democracy*. Schumpeter likened democratic governments that produced public policies to private firms that produced consumer and other products. Operators of private firms are not motivated by the desire to create specific products for society, but by the desire to create profits for themselves. Producing socially-useful products is the means by which they can attain their self-interested goal of making profits. Similarly, Schumpeter argued, politicians operating governments are not motivated by a desire to adopt or carry out specific public policies. Rather, their chief goal is to get elected so as to enjoy the power and other perquisites of office. The publicly-useful policies they advocate are simply the means by which they can attain their self-interested goal of gaining and keeping office.

This view was a radical departure from the theories of government motivation then prevailing among most economists and even among many political scientists. They contended that government officials were motivated by the desire to promote the public interest, not their own private interests. Therefore, entrusting some activity to the government automatically placed it in the hands of actors who would altruistically pursue the public interest. Those officials would not selfishly follow the type of self-interested motives that – according to prevailing economic theory – dominated private-sector decision-making among both consumers and firms. So most economic and many political theories of government decision-making focused on how to determine the public interest – often called 'maximizing public welfare'.

Schumpeter's iconoclastic idea was an appealing concept to explore, but the Social Science Research Council would not transfer my scholarship to it. So Kenneth Arrow, my thesis adviser, persuaded the Office of Naval Research to finance my thesis. I have never figured out how he convinced them that my doing so would benefit the US Navy, but I was grateful to him. I became even more grateful as he guided me through the writing of what turned out to be *An Economic Theory of Democracy*. Ken Arrow has the most brilliant and fastest-working mind I have ever encountered, and is also a wonderful adviser and a very supportive person.

However, *An Economic Theory of Democracy* might have remained an obscure Office of Naval Research manuscript if it were not for the generosity of Professor Ed Lindblom of Yale. He read a copy of my thesis and immediately persuaded three major publishers to send me signed contracts for its publication. I did not meet Ed Lindblom face-to-face until more than ten years later, but I am eternally grateful for his extending a helpful hand to an unknown graduate student whom he had never met. *An Economic Theory of Democracy* is still in print after 40 years, and produces more royalties each year than all my other books combined (unfortunately, that is not saying much!). It has sold at least 50 000 copies, been translated into several foreign languages and is one of the most frequently cited works in political science. No one could have been more surprised than I was – and still am.

Although *An Economic Theory of Democracy* is a purely theoretical book, not directly grounded in empirical research or data (it does not contain a single regression or other equation!), it does draw heavily upon my own personal experiences in student government at Carleton College, as noted above. My second book similarly drew heavily from my personal experiences – this time my three-year stint on active duty as an air intelligence officer in the US Navy. This occurred from 1956 to 1959, immediately after I finished my doctoral thesis. I left the Navy in 1959 and joined my father's consulting firm, Real Estate Research Corporation, in Chicago. In 1965, the Rand Corporation asked me to go to Santa Monica to analyse how bureaucracies make decisions.

Rand was puzzled by the seemingly irrational behaviour of two bureaucracies important to its existence: the Soviet military – its enemy – and the US Air Force – its sponsor. Rand wanted me to apply to bureaucracies the same almost cynical perspective about the behaviour of public officials – that they are significantly motivated by self-interest – that I had applied to political parties in *An Economic Theory of Democracy*. So my wife, our four childen and I moved to Santa Monica for two years. I worked partly for Rand and partly for the Los Angeles office of Real Estate Research Corporation, spending alternate weeks in each place. In about two years, I managed to write the book *Inside Bureaucracy*, which was published by Little Brown Inc. in 1967.

While I was serving in the US Navy, I often lamented that my time was being wasted. I did not begrudge giving three years to my country, but the billet assigned to me did not make any use of my training as an economist. Only when I started writing about bureaucracy some six years later did I realize that the Navy had been an outstanding training ground concerning how bureaucracies work. My position as a lowly intelligence lieutenant junior grade on an aircraft carrier enabled me to observe several layers of a military bureaucracy simultaneously, discovering how they interacted and what motivated their members.

That experience convinced me that no one version of how a bureaucrat thinks and acts could encompass the great variety of different behaviours I had seen in the Navy. Therefore, instead of assuming that all bureaucrats have the same motivations, I defined five different types of bureaucrats, each with a unique set of motives and behaviours. This approach defies the usual economics assumption that a single, totally abstract utility function can serve as a theoretical vessel into which individual variations in behaviour can be poured. But it enabled me to create a much more realistic model of how bureaucrats and bureaucracies behave than would assuming that all bureaucrats act alike. This model was also superior to assuming that all bureaucrats have abstract goal-structures so empty of specific contents (such as generalized 'utility functions') that very little about day-to-day behaviour can be deduced from them. I believe similar multiple utility-function assumptions would probably greatly improve theories of consumer behaviour, and perhaps even theories of firm behaviour, compared to the continued use of totally abstract utility functions assumed to be the same for all consumers or all firms.

After I returned to Chicago in 1965 to work full-time for Real Estate Research Corporation, my activities – and interests – shifted almost entirely to real estate and urban affairs. However, I was still determined to write about my experiences in ways that drew significant and broad underlying conclusions from detailed everyday activities. The consulting business offered many opportunities to do that. It constantly exposed me to new and different problems and issues connected with business and government policies concerning land uses and demographics. Insofar as possible, I tried to turn insights gained from specific consulting assignments into publishable articles. Some were collected in 1970 into a book of essays entitled *Urban Problems and Prospects*, published by Rand McNally; a second edition was published in 1976.

Another aspect of my personal experience crucially affecting my writing was serving as a principal consultant to the National Commission on Civil Disorders (the 'Kerner Commission'), which President Lyndon Johnson appointed to investigate the urban riots of 1967. I had previously had a slight acquaintance with Victor Palmieri, the Deputy Director of the Commission's staff. I managed to persuade him and David Ginsburg, the Director of the staff, that I already knew much about the subject they were going to investigate. My persuasiveness was based upon the fact that I had just finished serving with a secret Presidential Task Force on Cities, appointed in 1965 again by President Johnson and chaired by Paul Ylvisaker. For more than two years after the 1965 Watts Riots in Los Angeles, this task force had been analysing problems of large cities. We wrote a final report predicting that large-scale racial violence would break out in many big US cities if conditions in black neighbourhoods did not improve. President Johnson suppressed this report, not even showing it to Robert Weaver, then Secretary of Housing and Urban Development. But then the Newark and Detroit riots of early 1967 exploded. So the President appointed this new Commission to look publicly into exactly what the task force had been looking into secretly for two years. I was appointed to the Kerner Commission and, working nights and weekends for months, wrote the first drafts of four of the chapters in its final report – including the chapter on the future of American cities.

This experience convinced me – as well as many others – that the racial ghettos of America posed one of our society's central problems that needed to be addressed far more powerfully than in the past. That conviction motivated me to write two books focused on this subject. One was *Racism in America – And What to Do About It*, a long booklet written for the US Civil Rights Commission and published in 1970. It is heavily based upon the ideas of John McKnight. Because he was then on the staff of the Commission, he could not be listed as a co-author, as he should have been. The second book was *Opening Up the Suburbs*, published in 1973 by the Yale University Press. It sets forth a housing strategy reflecting my profound belief that inner-city problems cannot be resolved in the long run without reducing the sizable concentrations of very poor people – mostly minorities – found in the core areas of about 50 large American cities. The book advocates creating small scattered clusters of subsidized housing throughout American suburbs, enabling many low-income households from inner-city areas to move into those units if they so wish. It pre-dated the Gautreaux Experiment in Chicago which, in 1976, started doing just that through housing vouchers rather than new construction. That Experiment has successfully moved 5000 mainly-black households out of Chicago public housing into suburban and outer-city neighbourhoods.

Among all my writings, with the possible exception of my work for the Kerner Commission, *Opening Up the Suburbs* is the one I felt the most powerful pressure from my conscience to complete, even though I had no consulting assignments related to it. I still believe its extremely unpopular message is basically correct, although its strategy has been decisively rejected by most Americans.

The strategy of turning consulting assignments into publications if at all possible resulted in two other books published in 1973 by Lexington Press. One was *Federal Housing Subsidies: How Are They Working?*, written for the National Association of Homebuilders. The second was *Achieving Effective Desegregation*, an analysis of successful school desegregation tactics written by Leanne Lachman, Al Smith and myself for the Cabinet Committee on Education in the Nixon Administration.

In 1970, my father sold the Real Estate Research Corporation to the First Chicago Corporation, the parent holding company of the First National Bank of Chicago. I continued working at Real Estate Research for seven more years, becoming chairman in 1973 when health problems compelled my father to retire. At that time, I had worked for him for 14 years and my relationship with him profoundly shaped my life in almost every way. We were not only the best of friends, but he had a realistic grasp of both my capabilities and limitations. He never entrusted me with managerial responsibility for the firm. Yet he let me 'do my own thing' in terms of creative analysis methods, taking on entirely new types of assignments, and writing about them. Also, he stood behind me when I made controversial judgements about public policies, even when doing so cost the firm dearly in terms of lost business. One example was, in the early 1970s, our complete reform of the Cook County Assessor's Office – one of the largest in the nation. Having been put in charge of this politically sensitive assignment, I insisted on doubling assessed values of the houses in Mayor Richard J. Daley's home ward – over his vehement objections – in order to bring them into line with those in the rest of the County. The Mayor never forgave me for that – even though he had personally urged me to do whatever was necessary to clean up the Assessor's Office. Consequently, the City of Chicago stopped giving our firm business when it had previously been our largest client. Yet my father – a close friend and adviser to the Mayor – never said one word to me in criticism of that decision. He was a great citizen, a great father and a great man, and both an imaginative thinker and a successful entrepreneur. Because of him, I am a firm believer in the virtues of nepotism!

In 1977, after a conflict with the then head of First Chicago Corporation, I decided to leave the Real Estate Research Corporation. The Brookings Institution had previously asked me if I was interested in going there and, fortunately for me, that offer was still open, so I took it. The family moved to McLean, Virginia, just west of Washington. I agreed to work 80 per cent of the time for Brookings, while retaining the right to spend 20 per cent as a private consultant. This change allowed me far more time to devote to individual writing projects than I had ever enjoyed in a consulting firm – while still profiting from some public speaking and consulting.

Brookings is a terrific place in which to do policy-oriented research on public issues. It has a stellar reputation that ensures its members an audience with almost anyone, and is located in the midst of the Washington government policy world. It has a fine library and computer centre, a cafeteria in which staff members can mingle and exchange ideas, and above all, other staff members of unparalleled ability in many fields. Furthermore, it permits its senior fellows to focus on major policy-oriented projects, not all of which can be supported by outside funding. This fruitful environment has enabled me to write nine books (two with co-authors), co-edit two other books (with Katharine Bradbury) and publish over 200 articles in a 20-year period, during the last few years of which I have worked half-time or less for Brookings. The rest of the time I have made speeches around the nation (25–45 per year), served on boards of directors and have undertaken a few consulting assignments.

During the 1980s, when rampant conservatism in Washington drastically reduced interest in urban problems, I decided to shift the focus of my policy analysis from inner-city ghettos to the growth of suburbs and the relationship of that growth to inner-city problems. This is the subject of my book *New Visions for Metropolitan America* and also of my current research on the costs of suburban sprawl compared with the costs of alternative forms of metropolitan growth. These topics are likely to engage the attention of key public policy decision-makers for several decades to come.

What lessons can be drawn from all this experience for others interested in policy-oriented research and publication? The following seem most important:

- *Get personally involved in activities that provide direct experience in the fields you want to write about.* If you are not so involved, it is hard to know what is really happening. Reading the literature is not enough. Neither is sitting in your office and viewing the real world from afar. If you are not a practitioner, at least go around and interact with those who are *in their home territories.* Join their trade organizations or professional societies and attend their meetings. My constant speech-making around the nation is an invaluable source of ideas that I would never have encountered if I had not met people on their home grounds and discussed local conditions with them. I have been an active member of the Urban Land Institute for 20 years, rather than being active in the American Economic Association. Doing so enabled me to get to know the nation's major real estate developers, home-builders, providers of financing, consultants, and urban public officials, and to keep informed about what they are doing and thinking. There is no sub-stitute for such direct interactions with the people who are actually doing whatever is being done in each field of interest.
- *Tell the truth, no matter how unpopular it may be.* You do not have to be

tactless, but speaking the truth will often be so novel it will impress people with your originality. In Chicago in 1963, I wrote a housing analysis for the city that explicitly dealt with the process of neighbourhood racial transition from white to black that had dominated housing dynamics there for 20 years. Yet before then, neither race nor that neighbourhood transition process had ever been mentioned in any official city documents, so as to avoid contro-versy. The city government tried to suppress my study. But a reporter stole a copy from the Planning Department and printed it in daily instalments on the back page of the *Chicago Daily News*. This forced city officials at least to begin talking realistically about housing markets.

- *Write about how current and local events and trends are related to longer-run forces*. Many observers can describe what is happening on the surface, but few dig down deep enough to relate current events to long-run trends and forces.

- *Write clearly in easily-understood terms*. Most academic writers are not interested in communicating with real-world policy-makers. They only want to communicate with other academics who also understand esoteric-speak. Forget it! Use a simple word whenever a complicated one will do. Write in short sentences (though not always this short!). Break long sentences into shorter ones. If your teenage child can understand what you are saying, then it is probably clear enough. If not, keep re-writing.

- *Draw explicit conclusions about what is likely to happen and about the resulting policy implications – do not leave 'pulling it all together' up to your readers*. Analyses that conclude 'on the one hand, this, but on the other hand, that' are highly unsatisfying. If conclusions are implicit in your analysis, draw them yourself and explain them explicitly. That is why I am including this last section on lessons to be drawn!

- *Once you have generated a few really significant ideas, repeat them over and over in your writing and speaking*. Changing public opinion – even élite public opinion – about anything important is an immensely difficult task. It requires overcoming the massive inertia built into prevailing views by various self-interested structures and groups benefiting from those views. In truth, most influential thinkers and writers come up with only a small number of really good original ideas during a lifetime – a dozen would be a lot. To get those ideas widely accepted in our society of over 250 million persons requires broadcasting them constantly for years and years, perhaps changing their form slightly to disguise this repetition. Persistence – almost to the point of becoming an intellectual nuisance – is thus one of the most important virtues of an effective public policy analyst.

- *Recognize that true research consists of exploring the as-yet-unknown; so how you come out at its end may be quite different from what you expected at its beginning*. I have made an initial outline of every book I have started to write, but the finished products rarely followed those first outlines very closely. Whole sections planned at the outset were rejected along the way, and the need for entirely new sections always emerged. In two cases, a manuscript I had worked on for almost two years was judged inadequate by outside readers. I revised one and it became one of my more successful books; the other I put aside as needing a lot more work, and it may never see the light of day. That was a blow to my ego but, upon reflection, I concluded that the outside reviewers were right. A good researcher nearly always has some basic hypotheses at the outset, but must be willing to chance failing to substantiate those theories or any other interesting conclusions!

- *Do not shrink from advocating unpopular positions if you strongly believe you are right.* Most of the great advances in social policy throughout history have started out as unpopular views of a small minority. Examples are effective voting rights for almost every group from propertyless adult males to women to African-Americans, free education for everyone, social security systems, health insurance and pensions for workers, and freedom of religion. Policies that are almost inconceivable when first promoted often become almost universally accepted after many decades of advocacy and eventual adoption. Racial desegregation of public facilities is a recent example. Someone must carry the torch for such innovations during periods when most people reject them. Such a prophetic role is a vital function performed by enlightened social policy analysts. Carrying out this role calls for both persistence and courage in the face of strong opposition.

- *Do not take yourself so seriously that you omit all humour from your work – especially speeches or lectures.* Mosts academic treatises or speeches, even those about public policies, are deadly to encounter; they quickly cause the MEGO syndrome – 'My Eyes Glaze Over'! Just telling one joke at the outset of a speech is not adequate either. I have become notorious in real estate circles for illustrating my main points with jokes or stories; I try to tell one about every three or four minutes to keep the audience alert. Even my telephone answering machine message says 'Hi there! This is the world's leading authority speaking. I am too busy thinking great thoughts to come to the phone right now. But you know what to do, so just do it!' But to use humour successfully, you must take it rather seriously. I subscribe to several joke services; frequently buy and read joke books; and read all the stories in *The Reader's Digest*, which most of my audiences consider beneath their dignity to peruse. But all that effort has greatly enhanced my audience appeal.

One last lesson is probably the most important of all, but may be difficult for many people to follow today. It is to ground your life on fundamental foundations that will continuously replenish your enthusiasm, and sustain you when things get tough. My two strongest pillars have been my wife Kay and my religion. Before we married 41 years ago, Kay and I made an implicit pact: I would earn the money, and she would operate the household and do most of the rearing of the children. She could have been an outstanding career woman, since she was working on her Ph.D. when we were married. But she chose to concentrate on our family – at least until our fifth and last child was in high school, at which point she went to law school at the age of 50. Such a family-first focus was typical of very talented women in the 1950s. It is much rarer today; now most highly-educated women pursue their own professional careers while raising a smaller family with a lot more direct help from their husbands than I provided. Yet without her outstanding management of our home and children, plus her constant support and encouragement of my own efforts, I could never have devoted so much time to writing about the projects on which I was working. I am not necessarily recommending this pattern today, but I would be remiss not to mention how significant it has been in my own life. Unfortunately, my wife has recently contracted cancer, so I must now even more strongly emphasize my role as her key supporter. I hope I can do that half as well as she has always supported me.

Similarly, I have depended greatly upon faith in a power greater then ourselves. That faith sustains not only my personal life, but also my long-run persistence in promoting often unpopular public policies that I believe would improve society. I hope to keep working at that endless task for many more years to come.

References

Joseph A. Schumpeter (1950), *Capitalism, Socialism, and Democracy*, New York: Harper and Brothers.

Writings of Anthony Downs

An Economic Theory of Democracy (1957), New York: Harper and Brothers.
Inside Bureaucracy (1967), A Rand Corporation Research Study, Boston, MA: Little, Brown and Company.
Urban Problems and Prospects (1970), Chicago, IL: Markham Publishing Company.
Racism in America and How to Combat It (1970), Washington, DC: U.S. Civil Rights Commission, U.S. Government Printing Office.
Urban Problems and Prospects, Second Edition (1976), Chicago, IL: Rand McNally College Publishing Company.
Federal Housing Subsidies: How Are They Working? (1973), Lexington, MA: D.C. Heath and Company.
Opening Up The Suburbs: An Urban Strategy for America (1973), New Haven, CT: Yale University Press.
Neighborhoods and Urban Development (1981), Washington, DC: The Brookings Institution.
Stuck in Traffic (1992), Washington, DC: The Brookings Institution and the Lincoln Institute for Land Policy.
New Visions for Metropolitan America (1994), Washington, DC: The Brookings Institution and the Lincoln Institute of Land Policy.
A Reevaluation of Residential Rent Controls (1996), Washington, DC: The Urban Land Institute.
Achieving Effective Desegregation (1973), with A. Smith and M. Leanne Lachman, Lexington, MA: D.C. Heath and Company.

AN ECONOMIC THEORY OF POLITICAL ACTION IN A DEMOCRACY[1]

ANTHONY DOWNS

Chicago, Illinois

I

IN SPITE of the tremendous importance of government decisions in every phase of economic life, economic theorists have never successfully integrated government with private decision-makers in a single general equilibrium theory. Instead they have treated government action as an exogenous variable, determined by political considerations that lie outside the purview of economics. This view is really a carry-over from the classical premise that the private sector is a self-regulating mechanism and that any government action beyond maintenance of law and order is "interference" with it rather than an intrinsic part of it.[2]

However, in at least two fields of economic theory, the centrality of government action has forced economists to formulate rules that indicate how government "should" make decisions. Thus in the field of public finance, Hugh Dalton states:

As a result of [the] operations of public finance, changes take place in the amount and in the nature of the wealth which is produced, and in the distribution of that wealth among individuals and classes. Are these changes in their aggregate effects socially advantageous? If so the operations are justified; if not, not. The best system of public finance is that which secures the maximum social advantage from the operations which it conducts.[3]

A similar attempt to differentiate the operations "proper" to government from those "proper" to private agents has been made by Harvey W. Peck, who writes: "If public operation of an enterprise will produce a greater net social utility, the services rendered by this enterprise should belong in the category of public goods."[4] In addition, several welfare economists have posited general principles to guide government action in the economy. For example, Abba P. Lerner indirectly states such a rule when he says: "If it is desired to maximize the total satisfaction in a society, the rational procedure is to divide income on an equalitarian basis."[5]

Admittedly, this list of examples is not very long, primarily because overt statements of a decision rule to guide government action are extremely rare in economic theory. However, it does not unduly distort reality to state that most welfare economists and many public finance theorists implicitly assume that the "proper" function of government is to maximize social welfare. Insofar as they face the problem of government de-

[1] The argument presented in this article will be developed further in my forthcoming book, *An Economic Theory of Democracy*, to be published by Harper & Bros.

[2] See Gerhard Colm, *Essays in Public Finance and Fiscal Policy* (New York: Oxford University Press, 1955), pp. 6–8.

[3] *The Principles of Public Finance* (London: George Routledge & Sons, Ltd., 1932), pp. 9–10.

[4] *Taxation and Welfare* (New York: Macmillan Co., 1925), pp. 30–36, as quoted in Harold M. Groves (ed.), *Viewpoints in Public Finance* (New York: Henry Holt & Co., 1948), p. 551.

[5] *The Economics of Control* (New York: Macmillan Co., 1944), p. 32.

135

cision-making at all, they nearly all sub-scribe to some approximation of this normative rule.

The use of this rule has led to two major difficulties. First, it is not clear what is meant by "social welfare," nor is there any agreement about how to "maximize" it. In fact, a long controversy about the nature of social welfare in the "new welfare economics" led to Kenneth Arrow's conclusion that no rational method of maximizing social welfare can possibly be found unless strong restrictions are placed on the preference orderings of the individuals in society.[6]

The complexities of this problem have diverted attention from the second difficulty raised by the view that government's function is to maximize social welfare. Even if social welfare could be defined, and methods of maximizing it could be agreed upon, what reason is there to believe that the men who run the government would be motivated to maximize it? To state that they "should" do so does not mean that they will. As Schumpeter, one of the few economists who have faced this problem, has pointed out:

> It does not follow that the social meaning of a type of activity will necessarily provide the motive power, hence the explanation of the latter. If it does not, a theory that contents itself with an analysis of the social end or need to be served cannot be accepted as an adequate account of the activities that serve it.[7]

Schumpeter here illuminates a crucial objection to most attempts to deal with government in economic theory: they do not really treat the government as part of the division of labor. Every agent in the division of labor has both a private motive and a social function. For ex-ample, the social function of a coal-miner is removing coal from the ground, since this activity provides utility for others. But he is motivated to carry out this function by his desire to earn income, not by any desire to benefit others. Similarly, every other agent in the division of labor carries out his social function primarily as a means of attaining his own private ends: the enjoyment of income, prestige, or power. Much of economic theory consists in essence of proving that men thus pursuing their own ends may nevertheless carry out their social functions with great efficiency, at least under certain conditions.

In light of this reasoning, any attempt to construct a theory of government action without discussing the motives of those who run the government must be regarded as inconsistent with the main body of economic analysis. Every such attempt fails to face the fact that governments are concrete institutions run by men, because it deals with them on a purely normative level. As a result, these attempts can never lead to an integration of government with other decision-makers in a general equilibrium theory. Such integration demands a positive approach that explains how the governors are led to act by their own selfish motives. In the following sections, I present a model of government decision-making based on this approach.

II

In building this model, I shall use the following definitions:

1. *Government* is that agency in the division of labor which has the power to coerce all other agents in society; it is the locus of "ultimate" power in a given area.[8]

---

[6] *Social Choice and Individual Values* (New York: John Wiley & Sons, 1951).

[7] Joseph A. Schumpeter, *Capitalism, Socialism, and Democracy* (New York: Harper & Bros., 1950), p. 282.

[8] This definition is taken from Robert A. Dahl and Charles E. Lindblom, *Politics, Economics, and Welfare* (New York: Harper & Bros., 1953), p. 42. However, throughout most of my analysis the word "government" refers to the governing party rather than the institution as here defined.

2. A *democracy* is a political system that exhibits the following characteristics:

a) Two or more parties compete in periodic elections for control of the governing apparatus.

b) The party (or coalition of parties) winning a majority of votes gains control of the governing apparatus until the next election.

c) Losing parties never attempt to prevent the winners from taking office, nor do winners use the powers of office to vitiate the ability of losers to compete in the next election.

d) All sane, law-abiding adults who are governed are citizens, and every citizen has one and only one vote in each election.

Though these definitions are both somewhat ambiguous, they will suffice for present purposes.

Next I set forth the following axioms:

1. Each political party is a team of men who seek office solely in order to enjoy the income, prestige, and power that go with running the governing apparatus.[9]

2. The winning party (or coalition) has complete control over the government's actions until the next election. There are no votes of confidence between elections either by a legislature or by the electorate, so the governing party cannot be ousted before the next election. Nor are any of its orders resisted or sabotaged by an intransigent bureaucracy.

3. Government's economic powers are unlimited. It can nationalize everything, hand everything over to private interests, or strike any balance between these extremes.

4. The only limit on government's powers is that the incumbent party cannot in any way restrict the political freedom of opposi-

tion parties or of individual citizens, unless they seek to overthrow it by force.

5. Every agent in the model—whether an individual, a party or a private coalition—behaves rationally at all times; that is, it proceeds toward its goals with a minimal use of scarce resources and undertakes only those actions for which marginal return exceeds marginal cost.[10]

From these definitions and axioms springs my central hypothesis: political parties in a democracy formulate policy strictly as a means of gaining votes. They do not seek to gain office in order to carry out certain preconceived policies or to serve any particular interest groups; rather they formulate policies and serve interest groups in order to gain office. Thus their social function—which is to formulate and carry out policies when in power as the government—is accomplished as a by-product of their private motive—which is to attain the income, power, and prestige of being in office.

Getting votes

This hypothesis implies that, in a democracy, the government always acts so as to maximize the number of votes it will receive. In effect, it is an entrepreneur selling policies for votes instead of products for money. Furthermore, it must compete for votes with other parties, just as two or more oligopolists compete for sales in a market. Whether or not such a government maximizes social welfare (assuming this process can be defined) depends upon how the competitive struggle for power influences its behavior. We cannot assume a priori that this behavior is socially optimal any more than we can assume a priori that a given firm produces the socially optimal output.

---

[9] A "team" is a coalition whose members have identical goals. A "coalition" is a group of men who co-operate to achieve some common end. These definitions are taken from Jacob Marschak, "Towards an Economic Theory of Organization and Information," in *Decision Processes*, ed. R. M. Thrall, C. H. Coombs, and R. L. Davis (New York: John Wiley & Sons, 1954), pp. 188–89. I use "team" instead of "coalition" in my definition to eliminate intraparty power struggles from consideration, though in Marschak's terms parties are really coalitions, not teams.

[10] The term "rational" in this article is synonymous with "efficient." This economic definition must not be confused with the logical definition (i.e., pertaining to logical propositions) or the psychological definition (i.e., calculating or unemotional).

under perfect info.

I shall examine the nature of government decision-making in two contexts: (1) in a world in which there is perfect knowledge and information is costless and (2) in a world in which knowledge is imperfect and information is costly.

III

The analysis of government decision-making in a perfectly-informed world is intended only to highlight the basic relationship between a democratic government and its citizens. This relationship can be stated in the following set of propositions:

1. The actions of the government are a function of the way it expects voters to vote and of the strategies of its opposition.
2. The government expects voters to vote according to (a) changes in their utility incomes from government activity and (b) the strategies of opposition parties.
3. Voters actually vote according to (a) changes in their utility incomes from government activity and (b) the alternatives offered by the opposition.[11]
4. Voters' utility incomes from government activity depend on the actions taken by government during the election period.
5. The strategies of opposition parties depend on their views of the voters' utility incomes from government activity and on the actions taken by the government in power.

These propositions actually form a set of five equations containing five unknowns: expected votes, actual votes, opposition strategies, government actions, and individual utility incomes from government activity. Thus the political structure of a democracy can be viewed in terms of a set of simultaneous equations similar to those often used to analyze an economic structure.

[11] In a perfectly informed world, voters always vote exactly the way government expects them to, so the relationships expressed in Nos. 2 and 3 are identical. But in an imperfectly informed world, the government does not always know what voters will do; hence Nos. 2 and 3 may differ.

Because the citizens of our model democracy are rational, each of them views elections strictly as means of selecting the government most beneficial to him. Each citizen estimates the utility income from government action he expects each party would provide him if it were in power in the forthcoming election period; that is, he first estimates the utility income Party A would provide him, then the income Party B would provide, and so on. He votes for whatever party he believes would provide him with the highest utility income from government action. The primary factor influencing his estimate of each party's future performance is not its campaign promises about the future but its performance during the period just ending. Thus his voting decision is based on a comparison of the utility income he actually received during this period from the actions of the incumbent party and those he believes he would have received had each of the opposition parties been in power (I assume that each opposition party has taken a verbal stand on every issue dealt with concretely by the incumbents). This procedure allows him to found his decision on facts rather than on conjectures. Of course, since he is helping to choose a future government, he modifies his analysis of each party's past performance according to his estimate of probable changes in its behavior. Nevertheless, the current record of the incumbents remains the central item in his evaluation.

The government also makes decisions rationally, but its behavior is not so easy to analyze, because it is engaged in political warfare with its opponents. Each party resembles a player in an N-person game or an oligopolist engaged in cutthroat competition. However, the conjectural variation problem is somewhat simplified, because the incumbent party must always commit itself on each issue before the opposition parties do. Since it is in power, it must act whenever the occasion for a decision arises, if failure to respond is counted as a form of action. But the opposition, which is not responsible for the government, can wait until the pressure of events has forced the governing party to commit itself. Thus opposition parties have a strategic advantage —which incidentally makes the analysis of interparty warfare simpler than it would be if all parties revealed their strategies simultaneously.

However, I shall not explore party strategies in a perfectly informed world, because nearly all the conclusions that could be drawn are inapplicable to the imperfectly informed world in which we are primarily interested. Only one point should be stressed: in a world where perfect knowledge prevails, the government gives the preferences of each citizen exactly the same weight as those of every other citizen. This does not mean that its policies favor all citizens equally, since strategic considerations may lead it to ignore some citizens and to woo others ardently or to favor some with one policy and others with another. But it never deliberately eschews the vote of Citizen A to gain that of Citizen B. Since each citizen has one and only one vote, it cannot gain by trading A's vote for B's, *ceteris paribus*. In short, the equality of franchise is successful as a device for distributing political power equally among citizens.

IV

Lack of complete information on which to base decisions is a condition so basic to human life that it influences the structure of almost every social institution. In politics especially, its effects are profound. For this reason, I devote the rest of my analysis to the impact of imperfect knowledge upon political action in a democracy.

In this model, imperfect knowledge means (1) that parties do not always know exactly what citizens want: (2) that citizens do not always know what the government or its opposition has done, is doing, or should be doing to serve their interests; and (3) that the information needed to overcome both types of ignorance is costly—in other words, that scarce resources must be used to procure and assimilate it. Although these conditions have many effects upon the operation of government in the model, I concentrate on only three: persuasion, ideologies, and rational ignorance.

V

As long as we retain the assumption of perfect knowledge, no citizen can possibly influence another's vote. Each knows what would benefit him most, what the government is doing, and what other parties would do if they were in power. Therefore, the citizen's political taste structure, which I assume to be fixed, leads him directly to an unambiguous decision about how he should vote. If he remains rational, no persuasion can change his mind.

But, as soon as ignorance appears, the clear path from taste structure to voting decision becomes obscured by lack of knowledge. Though some voters want a specific party to win because its policies are clearly the most beneficial to them, others are highly uncertain about which party they prefer. They are not sure just what is happening to them or what would happen to them if another party were in power. They need more facts to establish a clear preference. By providing these facts, persuaders can become effective.

Persuaders are not interested per se in

selective info.

helping people who are uncertain become less so; they want to produce a decision that aids their cause. Therefore, they provide only those facts which are favorable to whatever group they are supporting. Thus, even if we assume that no erroneous or false data exist, some men are able to influence others by presenting them with a biased selection of facts.

This possibility has several extraordinarily important consequences for the operation of government. First, it means that some men are more important than others politically, because they can influence more votes than they themselves cast. Since it takes scarce resources to provide information to hesitant citizens, men who command such resources are able to wield more than proportional political influence, *ceteris paribus*. The government, being rational, cannot overlook this fact in designing policy. As a result, equality of franchise no longer assures net equality of influence over government action. In fact, it is irrational for a democratic government to treat its citizens with equal deference in a world in which knowledge is imperfect.

Access is critical

Second, the government is itself ignorant of what its citizens want it to do. Therefore it must send out representatives (1) to sound out the electorate and discover their desires and (2) to persuade them it should be re-elected. In other words, lack of information converts democratic government into representative government, because it forces the central planning board of the governing party to rely upon agents scattered throughout the electorate. Such reliance amounts to a decentralization of government power from the planning board to the agents.[12] The central board continues to decen-

tralize its power until the marginal vote-gain from greater conformity to popular desires is equal to the marginal vote-loss caused by reduced ability to co-ordinate its actions.

This reasoning implies that a democratic government in a rational world will always be run on a quasi-representative, quasi-decentralized basis, no matter what its formal constitutional structure, as long as communication between the voters and the governors is less than perfect. Another powerful force working in the same direction is the division of labor. To be efficient, a nation must develop specialists in discovering, transmitting, and analyzing popular opinion, just as it develops specialists in everything else. These specialists are the representatives. They exercise more power, and the central planning board exercises less, the less efficient are communication facilities in society.

The third consequence of imperfect knowledge and the resulting need for persuasion is really a combination of the first two. Because some voters can be influenced, specialists in influencing them appear. And, because government needs intermediaries between it and the people, some of these influencers pose as "representatives" of the citizenry. On one hand, they attempt to convince the government that the policies they stand for—which are of direct benefit to themselves—are both good for and desired by a large portion of the electorate. On the other hand, they try to convince the electorate that these policies are in fact desirable. Thus one of their methods of getting government to believe that public opinion supports them is to create favorable opinion through persuasion. Though a rational government will discount their claims, it cannot ignore them altogether. It must give the influencers

[12] Decentralization may be geographical or by social groups, depending upon the way society is divided into homogeneous parts.

unions, corporations, etc.

more than proportional weight in forming policy, because they may have succeeded in creating favorable opinions in the silent mass of voters and because their vociferousness indicates a high intensity of desire. Clearly, people with an intense interest in some policy are more likely to base their votes upon it alone than are those who count it as just another issue; hence government must pay more attention to the former than the latter. To do otherwise would be irrational.

Finally, imperfect knowledge makes the governing party susceptible to bribery. In order to persuade voters that its policies are good for them, it needs scarce resources, such as television time, money for propaganda, and pay for precinct captains. One way to get such resources is to sell policy favors to those who can pay for them, either by campaign contributions, favorable editorial policies, or direct influence over others. Such favor buyers need not even pose as representatives of the people. They merely exchange their political help for policy favors—a transaction eminently rational for both themselves and the government.

Essentially, inequality of political influence is a necessary result of imperfect information, given an unequal distribution of wealth and income in society. When knowledge is imperfect, effective political action requires the use of economic resources to meet the cost of information. Therefore, those who command such resources are able to swing more than their proportional weight politically. This outcome is not the result of irrationality or dishonesty. On the contrary, lobbying in a democracy is a highly rational response to the lack of perfect information, as is government's submission to the demands of lobbyists. To suppose otherwise is to ignore the existence

of information costs—that is, to theorize about a mythical world instead of the real one. Imperfect knowledge allows the unequal distributions of income, position, and influence—which are all inevitable in any economy marked by an extensive division of labor—to share sovereignty in a realm where only the equal distribution of votes is supposed to reign.

VI

Since the parties in this model have no interest per se in creating any particular type of society, the universal prevalence of ideologies in democratic politics appears to contradict my hypothesis. But this appearance is false. In fact, not only the existence of ideologies, but also many of their particular characteristics, may be deduced from the premise that parties seek office solely for the income, power, and prestige that accompany it.[13] Again, imperfect knowledge is the key factor.

In a complex society the cost in time alone of comparing all the ways in which the policies of competing parties differ is staggering. Furthermore, citizens do not always have enough information to appraise the differences of which they are aware. Nor do they know in advance what problems the government is likely to face in the coming election period.

Under these conditions many a voter finds party ideologies useful because they remove the necessity for relating every issue to his own conception of "the good society." Ideologies help him focus attention on the differences between parties; therefore, they can be used as samples of all the differentiating stands. Furthermore, if the voter discovers a correlation between each party's ideology

[13] I define "ideologies" as verbal images of "the good society" and of the chief policies to be used in creating it.

and its policies, he can rationally vote by comparing ideologies rather than policies. In both cases he can drastically reduce his outlay on political information by informing himself only about ideologies instead of about a wide range of issues.

Thus lack of information creates a demand for ideologies in the electorate. Since political parties are eager to seize any method of gaining votes available to them, they respond by creating a supply. Each party invents an ideology in order to attract the votes of those citizens who wish to cut costs by voting ideologically.[14]

This reasoning does not mean that parties can change ideologies as though they were disguises, putting on whatever costume suits the situation. Once a party has placed its ideology "on the market," it cannot suddenly abandon or radically alter that ideology without convincing the voters that it is unreliable. Since voters are rational, they refuse to support unreliable parties; hence no party can afford to acquire a reputation for dishonesty. Furthermore, there must be some persistent correlation between each party's ideology and its subsequent actions; otherwise voters will eventually eschew ideological voting as irrational. Finally, parties cannot adopt identical ideologies, because they must create enough product differentiation to make their output distinguishable from that of their rivals, so as to entice voters to the polls. However, just as in the product market, any markedly successful ideology is soon imitated, and differentiation takes place on more subtle levels.

[14] In reality, party ideologies probably stem originally from the interests of those persons who found each party. But, once a political party is created, it takes on an existence of its own and eventually becomes relatively independent of any particular interest group. When such autonomy prevails my analysis of ideologies is fully applicable.

Analysis of political ideologies can be carried even further by means of a spatial analogy for political action. To construct this analogy, I borrow and elaborate upon an apparatus first used by Harold Hotelling in his famous article, "Stability in Competition."[15] My version of Hotelling's spatial market consists of a linear scale running from zero to one hundred in the usual left-to-right fashion. To render it politically meaningful, I make the following assumptions:

1. The political parties in any society can be ordered from left to right in a manner agreed upon by all voters.
2. Each voter's preferences are single-peaked at some point on the scale and slope monotonically downward on either side of the peak (unless it lies at one extreme of the scale).
3. The frequency distribution of voters along the scale is variable from society to society but fixed in any one society.[16]
4. Once placed on the political scale, a party can move ideologically either to the left or to the right up to but not beyond the nearest party toward which it is moving.[17]
5. In a two-party system, if either party moves away from the extreme nearest it toward the other party, extremist voters at its end of the scale may abstain because they see no significant difference between the choices offered them.[18]

Under these conditions Hotelling's conclusion that the parties in a two-party system inevitably converge on the center does not necessarily hold true. If voters

[15] *Economic Journal*, XXXIX (1929), 41–57.

[16] Actually, this distribution may vary in any one society even in the short run, but I assume it to be fixed in order to avoid discussing the complex of historical, sociological, psychological, and other factors which cause it to change.

[17] It cannot go beyond the adjacent parties, because such "leaping" would indicate ideological unreliability and would cause its rejection by the electorate.

[18] This is equivalent to assuming elastic demand along the scale, as Smithies did in his elaboration of the Hotelling model (see Arthur Smithies, "Optimum Location in Spatial Competition," *Journal of Political Economy*, XLIX [1941], 423–39).

are distributed along the scale as shown in Figure 1, then Hotelling is right. Assuming that Party A starts at position 25 and Party B at 75, both move toward 50, since each can gain more votes in the center than it loses at the extremes because of abstention. But, if the distribution is like that shown in Figure 2, the two parties diverge toward the extremes rather than converge on the center. Each gains more votes by moving toward a radical position than it loses in the center.

This reasoning implies that stable government in a two-party democracy requires a distribution of voters roughly approximating a normal curve. When such a distribution exists, the two parties come to resemble each other closely. Thus, when one replaces the other in office, no drastic policy changes occur, and most voters are located relatively close to the incumbent's position no matter which party is in power. But when the electorate is polarized, as in Figure 2, a change in parties causes a radical alteration in policy. And, regardless of which party is in office, half the electorate always feels that the other half is imposing policies upon it that are strongly repugnant to it. In this situation, if one party keeps getting re-elected, the disgruntled supporters of the other party will probably revolt; whereas if the two parties alternate in office, social chaos occurs, because government policy keeps changing from one extreme to the other. Thus democracy does not lead to effective, stable government when the electorate is polarized. Either the distribution must change or democracy will be replaced by tyranny in which one extreme imposes its will upon the other.

Hotelling's original model was limited to the two-firm (or two-party) case, because, when three firms existed, the two

outside ones converged on the middle one, which then leaped to the outside to avoid strangulation. Since this process repeated itself endlessly, no stable equilibrium emerged. But, in my model, such leaping is impossible, because each party has to maintain continuity in its ideolo-

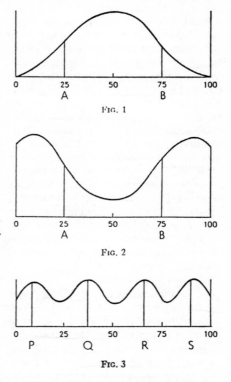

FIG. 1

FIG. 2

FIG. 3

gy. Hence this model can be applied to multiparty systems without resulting in disequilibrium.

Multiparty systems are most likely to exist when the distribution of voters is multimodal, as shown in Figure 3. A separate party forms at each mode, and each party is motivated to stay at its mode and to differentiate itself as completely as possible from its neighbors. If it moves to the left so as to gain votes, it loses just as many votes to the party on its right (or loses them because of abstention if it is an extremist party at the right end of the scale), and vice versa. Thus its optimal course is to stay where it is and keep other parties from approaching it. In a multiparty system, therefore, we find conditions exactly opposite to those in a viable two-party system. Whereas in the former each party links itself to a definite ideological position and stresses its differences from other parties, in the latter both parties move toward the political center so as to resemble each other as closely as possible.

This conclusion implies that voters in multiparty systems have a wider range of choice than voters in two-party systems and that each choice in this range is more definitely linked to some ideological position. Thus it appears that the electorate exercises a more significant function in a multiparty system than in a two-party system, because only in the former does it make much difference which party gets elected.

However, appearances are deceiving in politics, because in fact the government in a multiparty system is likely to have a less definite, less coherent, and less integrated program than the government in a two-party system. This paradoxical outcome arises from the necessity in most multiparty systems of forming coalition governments. Since voters are scattered among several modes, only rarely does one party obtain the support of a majority of those voting. Yet, in most democracies, the government cannot function without at least the indirect support of a majority of voters. Even in systems in which the legislature selects the government, a majority of its members must support the coalition chosen to govern before the coalition can take office. If we assume that representation in the legislature is "fair"—that each member represents the same number of citizens—then even a coalition government must receive the indirect support of a majority in order to govern.

Such support can be maintained only if the government implements at least some policies that appeal to—are ideologically near—each cluster of voters whose support it needs. If a majority of voters are massed in one relatively narrow band on the left-right scale, then the government can choose all its policies from within this band. Hence its policies will form a fairly cohesive set embodying the ideological viewpoint associated with that area of the scale. This outcome is typical of a two-party system.

But in a multiparty system there are many modes scattered across the whole scale. Therefore, in order to appeal to a majority of voters, the government must be a coalition of parties and must include in its policy-set some policies espoused by each party in the coalition. In this manner it "pays off" voters at each cluster in return for their support. However, the result is that its program contains policies reflecting a wide variety of ideological viewpoints, so that no real cohesion or integration about any one Weltanschauung is possible. This outcome necessarily occurs whenever the distribution of voters along the scale is so scattered that only a very wide band can encompass a majority.

Consequently, a multiparty system offers voters an ostensible choice between definite, well-integrated policy-sets in each election, but only rarely does one of these sets actually govern. Usually a coalition governs, and its policies are likely to be less definite and less well integrated than those of the government in a two-party system. This is true even though voters in the latter are offered only two relatively unintegrated alternatives which closely resemble each other. No wonder politics often seems confusing.

Whether a political system has two or more parties depends on the distribution of voters along the scale and on the electoral rules governing the system. To demonstrate this dual dependence, I use the concept of "political equilibrium." A state of political equilibrium exists when no new parties can successfully be formed and when no existing party is motivated to move away from its present position.

The limit to the number of new parties that can be formed successfully springs from my definition of success as ability to gain the income, power, and prestige that go with office; that is, as ability to get elected. If the constitution calls for the election of a legislature by proportional representation and the subsequent formation of a government by the legislature, then many parties can be formed, because any given party can get at least some of its members elected by winning the support of only a small proportion of the citizens. Once elected, these members have a chance to share in the fruits of office by joining a coalition government. Hence it follows from my hypothesis about party motivation that many parties are likely to exist in a proportional representation system. Their number is limited only by the number of seats in the legislature and by the necessity of formulating ideologies sufficiently different from those of existing parties to attract votes away from them.[19] New parties continue to form until the distribution of voters is "saturated"—until there is not enough ideological "room" between existing parties to support others significantly different from them.

In an electoral system in which a plurality is necessary for victory, the limit on successful party formation is much more stringent. Since the only way to insure a plurality against all opponents is to win a majority of votes, small parties tend to combine until two giants are left, each of which has a reasonable chance of capturing a majority in any given election. Where these two parties are located on the ideological scale depends upon the distribution of voters, as explained before.

Actually, the policy position and stability of the government in a democracy are relatively independent of the number of parties; they follow primarily from the nature of the distribution of voters along the left-right scale.[20] If a majority of voters are massed within a narrow range of that scale, democratic government is likely to be stable and effective, no matter how many parties exist. As noted earlier, the government can formulate a policy-set which appeals to a majority of voters and yet does not contain policies embodying widely disparate points of view. But, if the government can win the support of a majority only by adopting a scattering of policies chosen from a broad range of viewpoints, these policies tend to cancel each other out, and the government's net ability to solve social problems is low. Thus the distribution of voters—which is itself a variable in the long run—determines whether or not democracy leads to effective government.

VII

When information is costly, no decision-maker can afford to know everything that might possibly bear on his decision before he makes it. He must select

[19] The number of sufficiently different parties as system can support depends upon the shape of the distribution of voters along the scale.

[20] However, because the preferences of rising generations are influenced by the alternatives offered them, the number of parties is one of the factors that determine the shape of the distribution of voters.

only a few data from the vast supply in existence and base his decision solely upon them. This is true even if he can procure data without paying for them, since merely assimilating them requires time and is therefore costly.

The amount of information it is rational for a decision-maker to acquire is determined by the following economic axiom: It is always rational to perform any act if its marginal return is larger than its marginal cost. The marginal cost of a "bit" of information is the return foregone by devoting scarce resources— particularly time—to getting and using it. The marginal return from a "bit" is the increase in utility income received because the information enabled the decision-maker to improve his decision. In an imperfectly informed world, neither the precise cost nor the precise return is usually known in advance; but decision-makers can nevertheless employ the rule just stated by looking at expected costs and expected returns.

This reasoning is as applicable to politics as it is to economics. Insofar as the average citizen is concerned, there are two political decisions that require information. The first is deciding which party to vote for; the second is deciding on what policies to exercise direct influence on government policy formation (that is, how to lobby). Let us examine the voting decision first.

Before we do so, it is necessary to recognize that in every society a stream of "free" information is continuously disseminated to all citizens. Though such "free" data take time to assimilate, this time is not directly chargeable to any particular type of decision-making, since it is a necessary cost of living in society. For example, conversation with business associates, small talk with friends, reading the newspaper in a barber shop, and

listening to the radio while driving to work are all sources of information which the average man encounters without any particular effort to do so. Therefore, we may consider them part of the "free" information stream and exclude them from the problem of how much information a decision-maker should obtain specifically to improve his decisions.

The marginal return on information acquired for voting purposes is measured by the expected gain from voting "correctly" instead of "incorrectly." In other words, it is the gain in utility a voter believes he will receive if he supports the party which would really provide him with the highest utility income instead of supporting some other party. However, unless his vote actually decides the election, it does not cause the "right" party to be elected instead of a "wrong" party; whether or not the "right" party wins does not depend on how he votes. Therefore, voting "correctly" produces no gain in utility whatsoever; he might as well have voted "incorrectly."

This situation results from the insignificance of any one voter in a large electorate. Since the cost of voting is very low, hundreds, thousands, or even millions of citizens can afford to vote. Therefore, the probability that any one citizen's vote will be decisive is very small indeed. It is not zero, and it can even be significant if he thinks the election will be very close; but, under most circumstances, it is so negligible that it renders the return from voting "correctly" infinitesimal. This is true no matter how tremendous a loss in utility income the voter would experience if the "wrong" party were elected. And if that loss is itself small—as it may be when parties resemble each other closely or in local elections—then the incentive to become well informed is practically nonexistent.

Therefore, we reach the startling conclusion that it is irrational for most citizens to acquire political information for purposes of voting. As long as each person considers the behavior of others as given, it is simply not worthwhile for him to acquire information so as to vote "correctly" himself. The probability that his vote will determine which party governs is so low that even a trivial cost of procuring information outweighs its return. Hence ignorance of politics is not a result of unpatriotic apathy; rather it is a highly rational response to the facts of political life in a large democracy.

This conclusion does not mean that every citizen who is well informed about politics is irrational. A rational man can become well informed for four reasons: (1) he may enjoy being well informed for its own sake, so that information as such provides him with utility; (2) he may believe the election is going to be so close that the probability of his casting the decisive vote is relatively high; (3) he may need information to influence the votes of others so that he can alter the outcome of the election or persuade government to assign his preferences more weight than those of others; or (4) he may need information to influence the formation of government policy as a lobbyist. Nevertheless, since the odds are that no election will be close enough to render decisive the vote of any one person, or the votes of all those he can persuade to agree with him, the rational course of action for most citizens is to remain politically uninformed. Insofar as voting is concerned, any attempt to acquire information beyond that furnished by the stream of "free" data is for them a sheer waste of resources.

The disparity between this conclusion and the traditional conception of good citizenship in a democracy is indeed striking. How can we explain it? The answer is that the benefits which a majority of citizens would derive from living in a society with a well-informed electorate are indivisible in nature. When most members of the electorate know what policies best serve their interests, the government is forced to follow those policies in order to avoid defeat (assuming that there is a consensus among the informed). This explains why the proponents of democracy think citizens should be well informed. But the benefits of these policies accrue to each member of the majority they serve, regardless of whether he has helped bring them about. In other words, the individual receives these benefits whether or not he is well informed, so long as most people are well informed and his interests are similar to those of the majority. On the other hand, when no one else is well informed, he cannot produce these benefits by becoming well informed himself, since a collective effort is necessary to achieve them.

Thus, when benefits are indivisible, each individual is always motivated to evade his share of the cost of producing them. If he assumes that the behavior of others is given, whether or not he receives any benefits does not depend on his own efforts. But the cost he pays does depend on his efforts; hence the most rational course for him is to minimize that cost—in this case, to remain politically ignorant. Since every individual reasons in the same way, no one bears any costs, and no benefits are produced.

The usual way of escaping this dilemma is for all individuals to agree to be coerced by a central agency. Then each is forced to pay his share of the costs, but he knows all others are likewise forced to pay. Thus everyone is better off than he would be if no costs were borne, because everyone receives benefits which (I here assume) more than offset his share of the costs. This is a basic rationale for using coercion to collect revenues for national defense and for many other government operations that yield indivisible benefits.[21]

But this solution is not feasible in the case of political information. The government cannot coerce everyone to be well informed, because "well-informedness" is hard to measure, because there is no agreed-upon rule for deciding how much information of what kinds each citizen "should" have, and because the resulting interference in personal affairs would cause a loss of utility that would probably outweigh the gains to be had from a well-informed electorate. The most any democratic government has done to remedy this situation is to compel young people in schools to take courses in civics, government, and history.

Consequently, it is rational for every individual to minimize his investment in political information, in spite of the fact that most citizens might benefit substantially if the whole electorate were well informed. As a result, democratic political systems are bound to operate at less than maximum efficiency. Government does not serve the interests of the majority as well as it would if they were well informed, but they never become well informed. It is collectively rational, but individually irrational, for them to do so; and, in the absence of any mechanism to insure collective action, individual rationality prevails.

VIII

When we apply the economic concept of rationality to the second political use of information, lobbying, the results are

[21] See Paul A. Samuelson, "The Pure Theory of Public Expenditures," *Review of Economics and Statistics*, XXXVI (November, 1954), 387–89.

similarly incompatible with the traditional view of democracy. In order to be an effective lobbyist, a citizen must persuade the governing party that the policies he wants either are already desired by a large number of other citizens or are sufficiently beneficial to the rest of the electorate so that it will, at worst, not resent the enactment of these policies. To be persuasive, the would-be lobbyist must be extremely well informed about each policy area in which he wishes to exert influence. He must be able to design a policy that benefits him more than any other would, to counter any arguments advanced by opposing lobbyists, and to formulate or recognize compromises acceptable to him. Therefore, being a lobbyist requires much more information than voting, since even well-informed voters need only compare alternatives formulated by others.

For this reason, the cost of acquiring enough information to lobby effectively is relatively high. A lobbyist must be an expert in the policy areas in which he tries to exert influence. Since few men can afford the time or money necessary to become expert in more than one or two policy areas (or to hire those already expert), most citizens must specialize in a very few areas. Such behavior is rational even though policies in many areas affect them to some extent. Conversely, only a few specialists will actively exert pressure on the government in any one policy area. As a result, each need not heavily discount his own impact because of the large number of other persons influencing the decision, as he does in regard to voting. On the contrary, for those few lobbyists who specialize in any given area, the potential return from political information may be very high—precisely because they are so few.

The men who can best afford to become lobbyists in any policy area are those whose incomes stem from that area. This is true because nearly every citizen derives all his income from one or two sources; hence any government policy affecting those sources is of vital interest to him. In contrast, each man spends his income in a great many policy areas, so that a change in any one of them is not too significant to him. Therefore, men are much more likely to exert direct influence on government policy formation in their roles as producers than in their roles as consumers. In consequence, a democratic government is usually biased in favor of producer interests and against consumer interests, even though the consumers of any given product usually outnumber its producers. Tariff legislation provides a notorious example of this bias.

It should be stressed that such systematic exploitation of consumers by producers acting through government policy is not a result of foolish apathy on the part of consumers. In fact, just the opposite is true. Government's anticonsumer bias occurs because consumers rationally seek to acquire only that information which provides a return larger than its cost. The saving a consumer could make by becoming informed about how government policy affects any one product he purchases simply does not recompense him for the cost of informing himself—particularly since his personal influence on government policy would probably be slight. Since this is true of almost every product he buys, he adopts a course of rational ignorance, thereby exposing himself to extensive exploitation. Yet it would be irrational for him to act otherwise. In other words, lobbying is effective in a democracy *because* all the agents concerned—the exploiters, the exploited, and the government—behave rationally.

IX

Clearly, rational behavior in a democracy is not what most normative theorists assume it to be. Political theorists in particular have often created models of how the citizens of a democracy ought to behave without taking into account the economics of political action. Consequently, much of the evidence frequently cited to prove that democratic politics are dominated by irrational (non-logical) forces in fact demonstrates that citizens respond rationally (efficiently) to the exigencies of life in an imperfectly informed world.[22] Apathy among citizens toward elections, ignorance of the issues, the tendency of parties in a two-party system to resemble each other, and the anticonsumer bias of government action can all be explained logically as efficient reactions to imperfect information in a large democracy. Any normative theory that regards them as signs of unintelligent behavior in politics has failed to face the fact that information is costly in the real world. Thus political theory has suffered because it has not taken into account certain economic realities.

On the other hand, economic theory has suffered because it has not taken into account the political realities of govern-

[22] In this sentence the word "irrational" is not the opposite of the word "rational," as the synonyms in parentheses show. Admittedly, such dual usage may cause confusion. However, I have employed the word "rational" instead of its synonym "efficient" throughout this article because I want to emphasize the fact that an intelligent citizen always carries out any act whose marginal return exceeds its marginal cost. In contrast, he does not always make use of logical thinking, because, under some conditions, the marginal return from thinking logically is smaller than its marginal cost. In other words, it is sometimes rational (efficient) to act irrationally (non-logically), in which case an intelligent man eschews rationality in the traditional sense so as to achieve it in the economic sense. This is really what is meant by the sentence in the text to which this footnote is attached.

ment decision-making. Economists have been content to discuss government action as though governments were run by perfect altruists whose only motive was to maximize social welfare. As a result, economists have been unable to incorporate government into the rest of economic theory, which is based on the premise that all men act primarily out of self-interest. Furthermore, they have falsely concluded that government decision-making in all societies should follow identical principles, because its goal is always the maximization of social welfare. If my hypothesis is true, the goal of government is attaining the income, power, and prestige that go with office. Since methods of reaching this goal are vastly different in democratic, totalitarian, and aristocratic states, no single theory can be advanced to explain government decision-making in all societies. Nor can any

theory of government decision-making be divorced from politics. The way every government actually makes decisions depends upon the nature of the fundamental power relation between the governors and the governed in its society; that is, upon the society's political constitution. Therefore, a different theory of political action must be formulated for each different type of constitution.

I conclude that a truly useful theory of government action in a democracy—or in any other type of society—must be both economic and political in nature. In this article I have attempted to outline such a theory. If nothing else, the attempt demonstrates how much economists and political scientists must depend on each other to analyze government decision-making, which is the most important economic and political force in the world today.

[2]

WHY THE GOVERNMENT BUDGET IS TOO SMALL IN A DEMOCRACY

By ANTHONY DOWNS

IN a democratic society, the division of resources between the public and private sectors is roughly determined by the desires of the electorate. But because it is such a complex and time-consuming task to acquire adequate political information, the electorate is chronically ignorant of the costs and benefits of many actual and potential government policies. It is my belief that this ignorance causes governments to enact budgets smaller than the ones they would enact if the electorate possessed complete information. Yet these undersized budgets stem from rational behavior by both the government and the electorate; hence they are extremely difficult to remedy. Furthermore, the resulting misallocation of resources becomes more and more serious as the economy grows more complex.

As proof of these assertions, I shall present a model of a democratic society based upon the principles set forth in *An Economic Theory of Democracy*.[1] The basic rules for government and voter decision-making in this model are hypotheses, but the environment in which they are set resembles the real world as closely as possible. Furthermore, I believe the hypotheses themselves are accurate representations of what happens in the real world most of the time. My belief is based upon a comparison of the deductions made from these hypotheses in *An Economic Theory of Democracy* with the actual behavior of political parties in various democracies. However, the deductions made from the same hypotheses in this article are harder to compare directly with reality. Nevertheless, if the reader agrees with me that the basic hypotheses are realistic, it should follow that he will find the conclusions of this model meaningful in real-world politics as well as in the theoretical world of my argument.

This argument consists of the following topics: (1) how the budget is determined in a democracy, (2) the nature of rational political ignorance, (3) the definition of "correct" and "incorrect" budgets, (4) how an "incorrect" budget might arise, (5) significant differences between transactions in the public and private sectors, (6) distortions in budget evaluation arising from these differences, (7) a countertendency

---

[1] Anthony Downs, *An Economic Theory of Democracy*, New York, 1957.

toward overexpenditure, (8) the net results, and (9) the increasing importance of the problem.

I. How the Budget Is Determined in a Democracy

According to the economic theory of democracy, each government sets both expenditures and revenue collection so as to maximize its chances of winning the next election.[2] This follows from the axiom that political parties are primarily motivated by the desire to enjoy the income, prestige, and power of being in office. Each party regards government policies as means to these ends; hence it pursues whatever policies it believes will gain it the political support necessary to defeat its opponents. Since expenditures and taxes are two of the principal policies of government, they are set so as to maximize political support. Out of this rational calculation by the governing party comes the budget.

Rationality likewise prevails among voters. They vote for the party whose policies they believe will benefit them more than those of any other party.[3] These "benefits" need not be conceived in a narrowly selfish sense, but consist of any utility they derive from government acts, including acts which penalize them economically in order to help others.

The budget itself is not arrived at by considering over-all spending versus over-all taxation, but is the sum of a series of separate policy decisions. The governing party looks at every possible expenditure and tries to decide whether making it would gain more votes than financing it would lose. This does not mean that each spending bill is tied to a particular revenue bill. Instead all proposed expenditures are arranged in descending order of their vote-gain potential, and all proposed revenue collections arranged in ascending order of their vote-loss potential. Wherever these two marginal vote curves cross, a line is drawn that determines the over-all budget. Expenditures with a higher vote-gain potential than the marginal one are included in the budget, which is financed by revenue collection methods with lower vote-loss potentials than the marginal one.[4]

---

[2] For a complete explanation of this theory, see *ibid*. The government budget is discussed in chap. 4.

[3] The remainder of this article assumes a two-party system. Its conclusions are also applicable to multi-party systems, but the corresponding proofs are too complicated to be presented in an article of this length.

[4] This explanation of the budget process ignores the effect of government administrative bureaus upon the budget's final size. If self-aggrandizing bureaus were included in the model, each would try to maximize its own income, power, and prestige within the government. Hence it would submit a maximum estimate of its needs to the central budgeting agency (i.e., the directors of the governing party). The bureau might even

Because of the myriad expenditures made by modern governments, this rule may seem impractical. In the real world, it is true, the governing party does not weigh the vote impact of every single expenditure, but groups them into large categories like national defense. It then balances the marginal vote-gain of spending for each such category against its marginal vote-cost and against the marginal vote-gains of spending for other large categories, such as farm subsidies, education, and social security. Thus, in the real world, the aggregate budget for each category is decided in a manner similar to that described above, even though details of spending within the category may be left to non-political administrators.[5]

It should be noted that the government in our model never asks itself whether the over-all budget is "too large" or "too small" in relation to the views of the electorate. In fact, it never makes any explicit decision about what the over-all budget size should be, but determines that size merely by adding up all the items that more than pay for themselves

---

enlarge this estimate beyond its real needs in anticipation of the budgeting agency's desire to minimize expenditures. Its inflated requests would be bolstered by assertions that all of its spending would pay off well in votes. Since this process would distort the budgeting agency's information about what expenditures would in fact gain votes, the actual budget would tend to be larger than if bureaus were not self-aggrandizing. However, the central budgeting agency would be aware of the bureaus' inflationary tendencies and would develop outside checks against each bureau's vote-gain estimates. If the governing party failed to make such direct checks with the voters, it would be vulnerable to defeat by more alert opponents. Therefore, the information distortion caused by government bureaus could not be expected to offset the basic tendency for government budgets to be too small.

Another possible impact of administrative bureaus upon the model is their tendency to create situations in which their services are needed; e.g., by building missiles, the defense establishment of country A causes rival country B to counter with better missiles, thereby increasing the need for country A to spend even more money on missiles, etc. Robert K. Merton describes this process in "The Self-Fulfilling Prophecy" (chap. 7 of *Social Theory and Social Structure*, Glencoe, Ill., 1949). Since this characteristic of bureaus raises a whole set of fundamental problems beyond the scope of my model, I have made no attempt to account for it in this study. However, a model is under development which contains government administrative bureaus as a set of actors in addition to parties and voters. It is hoped that this model will shed further light on the effects of government bureaucracy.

[5] Some readers of this argument may object that spending for such categories as national defense cannot be evaluated in terms of votes but must be decided largely on technical grounds. I do not agree. For example, the United States government chose to abandon maintenance of strong conventional forces and stake the nation's entire defense upon the use of nuclear weapons. This decision was made against the technical advice of Army planners. From statements made by leading government officials at the time, it is clear that the decision was designed primarily to avoid asking the electorate to pay for both nuclear and conventional forces. In spite of the fact that every subsequent Army Chief of Staff has bitterly opposed this policy, the governing party has maintained it because the cost of its alternative is politically unpalatable. Thus in the real world, even regarding national defense, major budgetary questions are usually decided by vote possibilities.

in votes. Similarly, the voters do not evaluate a budget on the basis of its total size but by the particular benefits and costs it passes on to them.

The absence of any specific evaluation of over-all budget size appears to make our original assertion meaningless. How can we say the government budgets are too small when no one ever considers their size in judging them? The answer is that ignorance produces biases in the electorate that cause the government to exclude certain acts from the budget, thus reducing its size from what it "should be." Our original thesis can be more accurately stated as follows: rational ignorance among the citizenry leads governments to omit certain specific types of expenditures from their budgets which would be there if citizens were not ignorant. The fact that this results in budgets that are too small is simply a dramatic way of stressing the outcome.

II. Rational Political Ignorance

In this model, information is a crucial factor. In order to form policies, each party must know what the citizenry wants; and in order to vote rationally, each voter must know what policies the government and its opponents espouse. But in the real world, information is costly—if not in money, at least in time. It takes time to inform yourself about government policy. Furthermore, the number of policies that a modern government has to carry out is vast and their nature astoundingly complex. Even if the world's most brilliant man spent twenty-four hours a day reading newspapers and journals, he would be unable to keep himself well-informed about all aspects of these policies.

In addition to facing this problem, the average voter knows that no matter how he votes, there are so many other voters that his decision is unlikely to affect the outcome. This does not always prevent him from voting, because he realizes voting is essential to democracy and because it costs so little. But it usually does prevent him from becoming well-informed. Beyond the free information he picks up just by being alive in our media-saturated world, he does not see how acquiring detailed political data will make him better off. Thus a rationally calculating attitude about the use of time leads him to political ignorance. This conclusion is borne out by countless polls that show just how ignorant the average citizen is about major political questions of the day.

In this article we discuss three specific states of rational ignorance. The first is *zero ignorance*—i.e., perfect knowledge. In this state, citizens know (1) all actual or potential items in the budget of each party and (2) the full benefits and costs of each item. The second state is *partial ignorance*, in which voters know all the actual or potential items in the budget, but not all the benefits and costs attached to each item. Their political perception threshold has been raised so that remote or extremely complex events do not cross it, though the budget itself still does. The third state is *preponderant ignorance,* in which citizens are ignorant of both the items in the budget and their benefits and costs. In this state, citizens' perception thresholds are so high that they are aware of only the individual policies or items in the budget that vitally affect them.

III. "Correct" and "Incorrect" Budgets

My contention is that rational ignorance acts so as to produce an "incorrect" government budget. But what is meant by the term "incorrect" when the government does not seek to maximize welfare? Since I posit no social utility function, how can I say that one budget is "better" or "worse" than another except in terms of its vote-getting power? My answer is that the "correct" budget is the one which would emerge from the democratic process if both citizens and parties had perfect information about both actual and potential government policies. Insofar as an actual budget deviates from the "correct" budget, it is "incorrect." Admittedly, no one has perfect information; hence no one can say what budget would exist if there were no rational ignorance in politics. This fact prohibits use of the "correct" budget for detailed criticism of actual budgets, but it does not prevent generalizations about the tendency of actual budgets to deviate from "correct" budgets because of broad social factors like rational ignorance.

There is no point in denying that the terms "correct" and "incorrect" are ethical judgments. They presuppose that it is good for the citizens in a democracy to get what they want, and to base their wants on as much knowledge as possible. It is not good for them to get something they would not want if they knew more about it. That is the extent of my ethical foundation, and I think it is compatible with almost every normative theory of democracy.

IV. How an "Incorrect" Budget Might Occur

In a two-party democracy like ours, each national election can be considered a contest between two prospective government budgets. These budgets differ from each other in both quality and quantity, but each contains any spending and taxing measures about which there is strong majority consensus. In reality, many factors besides budgets influence people's political choices. However, most of these factors are in some way reflected in the budget, and in the rational world of economic theory we can assume that proposed budgets have a decisive role in determining how people vote. Knowing this, each party carefully plans its budget so as to maximize the support it gets, following the procedure described in Section I.

A key feature of this procedure is that the government gives voters what they want, not necessarily what benefits them. As long as citizens know what benefits them, there should be no difference between the actual budget and the "correct" budget. But if there are benefits which government spending would produce that people are not aware of, the government will not spend money to produce them unless it believes it can make them well-known before the next election. For the government is primarily interested in people's votes, not their welfare, and will not increase their welfare if doing so would cost it votes. And it would lose votes if it increased taxes or inflation—which people are aware of—in order to produce benefits which people are not aware of. Many citizens would shift their votes to some other party that produced only more tangible benefits at less total cost—even if they would in fact be worse off under this party.

Thus if voters are unaware of the potential benefits of certain types of government spending, party competition may force the actual budget to become smaller than the "correct" budget. This outcome may result even if voters merely discount certain classes of government benefits more heavily than comparable private benefits when in reality they are equal. Thus complete ignorance of benefits is not necessary to cause a "too small" budget—only relative unawareness of certain government benefits in relation to their cost, which under full employment consists of sacrificed private benefits.

Conversely, if citizens are less aware of certain private benefits than they are of government benefits, or if they see benefits more clearly than costs, the actual budget may tend to exceed the "correct" budget. In either case, ignorance causes a distorted evaluation of the relative benefits of public and private spending. This distortion is carried over into the budget by interparty competition, which forces each party to give voters what they want—not necessarily what the parties think would benefit them. Thus the ignorance of the voters may cause the actual budget to deviate from the "correct" budget.

Whether the actual budget is too large or too small depends upon the specific forms of ignorance present in the electorate. Since ignorance influences voters' thinking by distorting their evaluation of public vs. private spending, we must study the way citizens view these two types of spending before analyzing the net impact of ignorance upon the budget.

V. Significant Differences Between Transactions in the Public and Private Sectors

There are two significant differences between transactions in the private sector and in the public sector that are relevant to our analysis. First, in the private sector nearly all transactions are made on a *quid pro quo* basis, whereas in the public sector benefits are usually divorced from the revenues that make them possible. Whenever a citizen receives a private benefit, he pays for it directly and individually. Conversely, whenever he pays someone in the private sector, he receives a corresponding benefit which he has freely chosen because he wants it. No such direct link between costs and benefits exists in the public sector. Taxes are not allocated to individuals on the basis of government benefits received but on some other basis, usually ability to pay. Thus receipt of a given benefit may have no connection whatever with payment for it. And when a man pays his income tax or the sales tax on his new car, he cannot link these acts of sacrifice to specific benefits received. This divorce of benefits from payment for them makes it difficult to weigh the costs and benefits of a given act and decide whether or not it is worthwhile, as can be done regarding almost every private transaction.

There are two reasons why governments do not operate on a *quid pro quo* basis. First, the collective nature of many government benefits makes it technically impossible. For example, take national defense, which is the largest single item of government spending in most democracies.[6] But the benefits of national defense are collective in nature; that is, if they exist for one man, all men enjoy them. This fact makes *quid pro quo* transactions impossible, because once the benefit exists, enjoyment of it cannot be denied to those citizens who have not paid for it. For this reason, voluntary payment cannot be used to finance collective benefits. Since each citizen benefits whether or not he has paid, he maximizes his income by dodging his share of the cost. But *everyone* has this cost-minimizing attitude; so if voluntary payment is relied upon, no one pays. Consequently the resources necessary to provide the collective good are not provided, and no one receives any benefits. To avoid this outcome, individuals agree to coerce each other into payment through a collective agency like the government.

---

[6] In the United States, defense expenditures by the federal government constitute over 40 per cent of the total spending by all federal, state, county, local, and other government units. This figure applies to 1954 and is taken from U.S. Department of Commerce, *Statistical Abstract of the United States: 1956*, p. 401.

A second reason why governments do not use *quid pro quo* trans-actions is their desire to redistribute income. In the private sector, benefits are furnished only to those who can pay for them, or through voluntary charitable activities. But most modern democracies have elected to provide their poorest citizens with more benefits than those citizens can afford individually. This goal requires a deliberate violation of the *quid pro quo* relationship; poor citizens get more benefits than they pay for, and their richer brethren are forced to give up more in taxes than is spent on benefits for them. One way to accomplish such redistribution and at the same time allocate the costs of collective goods is to tax on the basis of ability to pay. Thus for both technical and ethi-cal reasons, the benefit principle that prevails in the private sector is largely abandoned in the public sector.

The second major difference between transactions in the private and public sectors is the coercive nature of dealings in the latter. Whereas all private transactions are voluntary, most payments to governments—other than direct sales of services—are enforced by law. Even the receipt of collective benefits is involuntary, since they exist whether a given citizen wants them or not. As noted, coercion is necessary because there is no intrinsic link between benefits and payments as in the private sector. Instead, force supplies this link.

But the use of force makes doing business with the government an all-or-nothing proposition. In the private sector, a citizen can enter into those transactions he desires and refrain from those he does not desire. No such selectivity is possible in his dealings with government. He must pay taxes that are used to pay for many projects he does not want. True, he can avoid taxes to some extent by directing his activities into untaxed areas; e.g., by refusing to buy luxury goods or cutting down the time he works. He can also exercise similar limited selectivity in receiv-ing government benefits. But by and large, since his payments to the government are not related to the benefits he receives from it, he finds himself contributing to things that do not benefit him. The result is that no one ever attains marginal equilibrium in his dealings with the government.

For a citizen, such equilibrium exists when the utility produced by that act of government which is least attractive to him (i.e., the "last" government act on his preference scale) is equal to the utility of the least attractive act he undertakes in the private sector (i.e., the "last" completed private act on his preference scale). Furthermore, there must be no additional government acts that would give him more utility than those now being carried out. Under these circumstances, the individual cannot be made better off by shifting resources from the private to the public sector or vice versa, or by any reallocation of resources within the public sector. (We assume he has already allocated his resources within the private sector to his maximum benefit.) This situation corresponds to equilibrium within the private sector as portrayed by classical economists—a state attained by utility-maximizers in a world of perfect competition.

However, even if perfect competition exists, the requirements for attaining perfect equilibrium with a democratic government are highly restrictive. If a majority of citizens have identical preference rankings of both public and private acts, then the government's actual policies will be just what those citizens want (assuming the government knows what their preference rankings are). The division of resources between public and private sectors will be precisely that necessary to assure the majority a state of equilibrium between the sectors.

But, in the real world, people's preference rankings are not identical, so we shall not assume them identical in our model. While almost every man agrees with a majority of his fellows in regard to some policies, he also finds himself in a minority regarding others. It is the presence of these "revolving majorities" that prevents men from attaining equilibrium with governments. The government must carry out a complex mixture of many policies, some pleasing to one majority, some pleasing to another majority, and some pleasing only to a minority with intensive feelings concerning them. It can afford to undertake policies favored only by a minority because it does not stand or fall on any one issue but on the mixture as a whole.[7] If society is at all complex, the government's gigantic policy mix is bound to contain at least one act which any given voter opposes. It is either positively repugnant to him (i.e., it produces negative utility apart from its resource-cost), or else he knows of better uses to which the resources it absorbs could be put. As long as only one such act exists for him, he is out of equilibrium with government. Even if we assume declining marginal utility of income in both private and public sectors, there is always some additional private use of resources (including charity) which would yield him positive utility. There may also be other government acts, not now being performed, which would yield him even more utility than the best private act he can think of. Hence his disequilibrium does not necessarily imply a desire to shift resources from the public to the private sector. It may

---

[7] Where the government does stand or fall on every issue, as in the French Fourth Republic, it can function successfully only if strong consensus exists among the majority. Otherwise it is continually defeated by "Arrow problems." See Downs, *op.cit.*, chap. 4.

also imply desire for reallocation within the public sector or even for moving more resources into that sector. But, in any case, there is always some change in government policy that would benefit him. Furthermore, the government is always spending money on projects he dislikes; hence his welfare would be improved if those projects were eliminated and his taxes reduced. *Therefore every citizen believes that the actual government budget is too large in relation to the benefits he himself is deriving from it.* Even if he feels the optimum budget would be much larger than the actual one, he believes the actual one could be profitably reduced "through greater economy"—i.e., elimination of projects from which he does not benefit.[8]

But if everyone feels the government is spending too much money for the benefits produced, why don't political parties propose smaller budgets? How can budgets which everyone regards as too large keep winning elections? The answer lies in the nature of the "revolving majorities" discussed previously. According to the economic theory of democracy, governments never undertake any policies unless they expect to win votes (or at least not lose votes) by doing so. Hence for every citizen opposed to a given act, there are other citizens in favor of it. Elimination of that act would please the former but alienate the latter. Looking at the whole complex of its acts between elections, the governing party feels that including this act gains more votes than excluding it. The party can afford to offend some voters with this act because they are in the minority regarding it, their feelings against it are not as intensive as the feelings of those for it, some other acts will placate them, or for some combination of these reasons. Since citizens' preferences are diverse, every man finds himself thus ignored by the government on some policy or other. Hence everyone believes the government is carrying out some unnecessary acts. But the government is still maximizing political support for itself, for what one man believes unnecessary is to someone else necessary enough to cause him to thank the government with his vote.

[8] This sentence appears to contradict the one preceding it, but in reality they are perfectly consistent. To illustrate, assume that an urban citizen pays $500 per year in taxes toward a government budget which is spent entirely for farm subsidies. Because he has no interest in farm subsidies, he thinks the budget is too large in relation to what he is getting out of it. However, he strongly desires urban renewal, and would be happy to pay $1,000 per year in taxes if the government budget were spent entirely on urban renewal. Thus, in his eyes, the actual budget is simultaneously too large and too small, depending on what alternative it is compared with. It is too large compared with a budget in which those expenditures he dislikes have been eliminated and all others remain the same. Yet it is too small in comparison with a budget in which the expenditure pattern has been changed to what he regards as optimum.

However, the resulting disequilibrium puts tremendous pressure on the government to reduce the budget wherever it can. This means it will make only those expenditures which produce benefits that voters are aware of, for hidden benefits cannot influence votes. Thus the threat of competing parties prevents the government from giving citizens what is good for them unless they can be made aware of the benefits involved before the next election. Only if a party has immense confidence in its ability to win the next election anyway is it free to produce such hidden benefits, no matter how important they are in the lives of the voters. The more "perfect" the competition between parties, the more closely must the government follow popular opinion, and the more likely it is to include in its policies any errors in that opinion caused by ignorance.

VI. Distortions in Budget Evaluation Arising from These Differences

Having analyzed the relevant differences between transactions in the public and private sectors, we now turn to the distortions they produce in benefit-appraisal. Such distortions are of two main types: underevaluation of government benefits in comparison with private benefits, and underevaluation of government cost in comparison with private cost. In both cases, the distortion occurs in estimating the government's contribution or cost rather than that of the private sector. This is true because the *quid pro quo* relationship in the private sector makes accurate estimation of both costs and benefits almost universal. Of course, some private spending is speculative in nature; e.g., people may attend a play not knowing beforehand whether it will be worth the price of admission. But because each private transaction is voluntary, purely individual in nature, and based on *quid pro quo* relations, the persons making it usually know its benefits and costs in advance (except in cases of financial speculation). The absence of these qualities in public transactions gives rise to two major sources of error.

(1) REMOTENESS

Benefits from many government actions are remote from those who receive them, either in time, space, or comprehensibility. Economic aid to a distant nation may prevent a hostile revolution there and save millions of dollars and even the lives of American troops, but because the situation is so remote, the average citizen—living in rational political ignorance—will not realize he is benefiting at all. Almost every type of preventive action, by its nature, produces such hidden benefits. People are not impressed with their gains from water purification, regulation of food and drugs, safety control of airways, or the regulation of utility and transport prices, unless these actions fail to accomplish their ends. Then, perhaps for the first time, the absence of effective protection makes them aware of the benefits they were receiving when it was present.

In contrast, the immediate benefits of almost all private goods are heavily emphasized. In order to sell these goods on a voluntary basis, their producers must convince the public of their virtues. Thus consumers are subject to a continuous advertising barrage stressing the joys of private goods, whereas no comparable effort dramatizes the benefits they receive from government action. Even private goods with benefits of a remote nature, such as cemetery lots, are advertised in such a way as to make awareness of these benefits immediate.

Furthermore, much of the cost of remote government benefits is not equally remote. In the private sector, the *quid pro quo* balancing of costs and benefits is often attenuated by time-payment plans which magnify benefits in relation to costs. But in the public sector the opposite is true. The major source of federal government revenue—personal and corporate income taxes—must be computed by taxpayers on an annual basis. Even if these taxes are paid by installments, the fact that each taxpayer must sit down and figure out exactly how much he has to pay each year makes this cost very real to him. His rational political ignorance does not insulate him equally from knowledge of government benefits and their costs, but it tends to emphasize the latter.

In some cases, this asymmetry is reversed. Sales taxes which are passed on to consumers are not strongly felt by them because they are spread over time in a series of relatively small payments, and each consumer does not annually add up his total payments. But the intermediate agent—e.g., the retailer who collects the sales tax—does compute the total amount paid. True, he realizes that this cost is borne by his customers in the long run.[9] Nevertheless, both his short-run interests and his ignorance tend to emphasize the government's acquisition of these resources rather than the benefits they eventually provide; hence this acquisition takes on the elements of confiscation.

The confiscatory cast of taxation is an inevitable result of the divorce of costs from benefits and the remoteness of the latter. Whereas in *quid pro quo* transactions each yielding of resources is justified by immediate receipt of benefits, taxation appears to be outright seizure of privately

---

[9] If competition is not perfect, he bears some of the cost himself. This fact strengthens the argument that citizens are relatively aware of the sacrifices imposed upon them by taxes, even indirect ones.

produced resources. It thus seems parasitic, rather than self-supporting like other costs of production or consumption. True, a rational taxpayer knows that he receives benefits in return for his taxes, but the remoteness of many such benefits removes the appearance of tit-for-tat balance that is present in private transactions.

In summary, a major portion of government benefits is remote in character compared with either taxes or private benefits. Since citizens are rationally ignorant of remote political events, they fail to realize all the government benefits they are receiving. However, they are well aware of a greater percentage of the taxes they pay and of the private benefits they are sacrificing to pay them. Because of this imbalance, the governing party cannot spend as much money on producing remote benefits as their real value to the citizenry warrants. Every dollar raised by taxation (or inflation) costs votes which must be compensated for by votes won through spending. But when the spending produces benefits that are not appreciated by voters, no compensating votes are forthcoming. Hence such spending must be restricted, or else the competing party will gain an advantage by cutting its own (proposed) spending and charging the incumbents with "waste." True, if the incumbents can demonstrate to the voters that this spending actually produces valid benefits, such charges will be harmless. But such demonstrations absorb resources themselves, especially since the nature of remote benefits makes them hard to document. And since the government is under constant pressure to cut expenditures, it cannot afford to use resources advertising the benefits of its policies. In this respect, it differs from private concerns, which must advertise in order to encourage voluntary purchase of their products. A striking example of this advertising asymmetry is in the field of electric power. Whereas private power corporations advertise both the virtues of their own product and the evils of public power, government utilities cannot even advertise their existence for fear of being accused of wasting public funds.

The outcome is a tendency toward elimination from the budget of all expenditures that produce hidden benefits. Only if the benefits involved are necessary for the survival of democracy itself will the governing party risk losing votes by producing them and spending resources to justify its actions. Even in this case, it tends to get by with the minimum possible amount because it fears charges of "waste" from its opponents.[10] Clearly, this situation causes government budgets to be

[10] This is not to deny that there is a great deal of actual waste in government which justly deserves censure. However, many political charges of "waste" are really attacks on production of genuine—but remote—benefits. These attacks are designed to capitalize

smaller than they would be if voters were perfectly informed about all benefits and costs, however remote.

(2) UNCERTAIN NATURE OF GOVERNMENT BENEFITS

Closely akin to remoteness is the uncertain nature of many government benefits compared with private ones. Since government must deal with factors affecting society as a whole, the problems it faces are much more complex than the problems facing individuals in their private lives. Many policies undertaken by governments are launched without either control or knowledge of exactly what their outcomes will be. This is particularly true in international relations or fields of rapid obsolescence, such as national defense. Here the future is so beset by unknowns that whether a given policy will produce benefits or penalties is often problematical, and appraisal of the expected value of benefits forthcoming is extremely difficult. In contrast, each citizen in his private life knows of many ways to invest resources which will give him immediate benefits. True, life is full of risks, and the future is unknown to individuals as well as governments. Nevertheless, each person faces a much simpler set of choices in his own life, with many fewer parameters, than does even a local government. Hence the returns from investing resources privately must be discounted much less than those from investing resources publicly.

This situation is not a result of rational political ignorance, but of the uncertainty inherent in any complex situation involving human action. Even the best-informed government experts cannot predict the outcome of many of their policies. They have plenty of current information, but do not understand all the basic forces at work, and cannot predict the free choices of the men involved. This kind of ignorance cannot be removed by greater personal investment in political information.

Again, the outcome is a budget smaller than the "correct" one. Because voters are led by rational ignorance to undervalue benefits from policies with uncertain outcomes, the government cannot count on gaining political support by spending money on these policies. But since it can count on losing support by raising the money, it tends to eschew such policies altogether.

Throughout the preceding argument, it is assumed that citizens' ignorance conceals benefits lost through failure to spend, but does not conceal losses of utility through excessive spending. Perhaps if citizens be-

on rational ignorance for political gain at the expense of the actual benefit of the citizenry.

came better informed about government policy, they would discover that present policies produce fewer benefits than they had supposed. In that case, increased information might increase their reluctance to transfer resources into the public sector. In other words, they would discover that the actual budget was larger than the "correct" budget instead of smaller.

This objection to our previous conclusion ignores the motivation of the government in regard to expending resources. Essentially, the argument implies that government conceals a great deal of "waste" spending under the cloak of citizens' ignorance; therefore if citizens had perfect information, they would want the government to eliminate this waste. Naturally, in a world of imperfect knowledge, every government makes mistakes, and undoubtedly perfect information would reveal such errors and cause the electorate to desire corrective reallocations. But, aside from this failing, the government has no motive to spend resources without producing tangible benefits. As we have seen, government policies are designed to gain votes by producing definite benefits known to voters. Furthermore, because voters are aware of the costs imposed upon them by government action, government is always under pressure to eliminate policies that do not justify their costs by producing tangible benefits. Hence it is irrational for government to "waste" resources on non-benefit-producing policies, since they lose votes through adding to taxation but do not gain votes by adding to benefits. Such "waste" expenditures would be rational only if (1) the government had a secondary motive of maximizing expenditures *per se* in addition to maximizing its chances for election, or (2) in the process of winning votes, the government spent money to benefit minorities in hidden ways which the majority would repudiate if they had perfect knowledge. The first case posits a government markedly different from the one in our model. Exploration of the behavior of such a government might be very interesting, but it cannot be undertaken in this article.[11] The second case will be dealt with in the next section.

[11] In my opinion, the elected officials of a democratic government are not significantly motivated to maximize expenditures. Their primary rewards are the perquisites of holding an elective office, and their attention and energies are focused upon overcoming the difficulty of remaining in that office in spite of challenges in every election. However, permanent bureaucratic functionaries in large governments do not have their energies absorbed by the problem of retaining their jobs. Hence they can concentrate on increasing their significance through expanding the size and influence of the departments under them, which usually involves increasing the amount of resources they control. Thus whether the expenditure-maximizing assumption enters a model of democratic government depends upon whether government in the model is simply a team of elected officials, or is a team of elected officials *plus* a set of permanent bureaucrats. The impact of the latter assumption has already been discussed in footnote 4.

VII. THE TENDENCY TOWARD EXCESSIVE SPENDING

Up to this point we have discussed two states of information in the electorate: perfect knowledge and partial ignorance. We have shown that when the latter prevails, costs of government action will appear more significant than benefits; so the actual budget will be smaller than the "correct" budget. However, there is also a third state of information: preponderant ignorance. In this state, citizens are ignorant of both the items in the budget and their benefits and costs. The budget that results when such ignorance predominates differs radically from those discussed previously: it tends to be *larger* than the correct size because of voters' ignorance of what items are in the budget.[12]

Government action affects each citizen in many ways, touching nearly all the functional "roles" he plays in society. Two important such roles are those of income-earner and consumer. As an income-earner, each citizen benefits when government spending increases the demand for the service he produces and when his taxes are reduced. He suffers when such spending is diminished or when his taxes increase. As a consumer, he suffers whenever government action increases the prices of the goods and services he buys, and he gains when it causes them to fall relative to his income.

Thus government action influences his welfare in both roles, but the two influences are not equally significant to him. Since almost every citizen receives nearly all his income from one source, any government act pertinent to that source is extremely important to him. In contrast, he spends his income on many products, each one of which absorbs a relatively small part of his total budget. Thus a government act which influences one of the products he consumes is nowhere near as vital to him as an act which influences the product he sells.[13] Under conditions of preponderant ignorance, this asymmetry means he is much more aware of government policies that affect him as an income-earner than he is of policies that affect him as a consumer.[14]

[12] However, this is not the only distortion caused by preponderant ignorance. It also encompasses the previously described tendency to create budgets that are too small because voters are ignorant of remote government benefits. The net effect of these two opposing forces is discussed in Section VIII.

[13] Many citizens sell their time and labor rather than an objective product. They are therefore interested in policies which affect both (1) the sale of their labor and (2) the sale of the particular products their labor is used to create.

[14] The classic example of this asymmetry is the tariff. A few producers manage to get government to set protective tariffs at the expense of millions of consumers, even though politicians seek to maximize votes. This is possible because producers are much more intensely interested in their income than consumers are in the individual prices that face them. See Downs, *op.cit.*, pp. 253-57.

GOVERNMENT BUDGET IN A DEMOCRACY

In order to maximize its political support, the government takes account of this situation in planning its budget. It realizes that two excellent ways to gain a citizen's support are to raise his income by giving him something for nothing or to buy what he produces. In some cases, both can be combined in a single act, such as hiring workers to build a public swimming pool which they subsequently use free of charge. But in a society with a complex division of labor, each specific income-earning group is usually a small minority of the population. Therefore government acts designed to please such a group usually distribute benefits to a minority, whereas their costs are added to the general tax burden and spread over the majority. Each recipient of such a boon thus feels he is making a net gain, since his share of the taxes added to pay for this project is much smaller than the benefit he receives. But the government also provides similar projects benefiting other minorities to which he does not belong. The costs of these projects are likewise spread over all citizens—including him—so he winds up paying for other people's special benefits, just as they pay for his. Whether or not he makes a net gain from this process is a moot point.

However, he cannot expect the government to undertake only those special projects which benefit him. Since a majority of citizens would be net losers under such an arrangement, they would vote against it. In order to get them to help pay for acts which benefit him, the government must provide them with benefits for which he helps to pay. Thus the government placates the majority who are exploited by a minority in one field by allowing them to be part of exploiting minorities in other fields.

In this process of "log-rolling," the citizens affected do not enter into direct bargains with each other. The only decision they face is which of the two competing budgets to vote for at each election. All the intervening trading of political support is done within the governing party, which knows that it must present the end result to the voters as a single package in competition with a similar package offered by its opponents. Each voter must then decide which budget provides him with the greatest difference between benefits received and costs imposed. If he receives many benefits from "special-interest" projects, he can expect his taxes to be swelled by the costs of similar projects benefiting other minorities, which the government must undertake to "buy off" the people who paid for his gains. Thus he might be better off if all minority benefits were eliminated and taxes lowered for everyone.

However, the question facing us is not whether budgets will include many or few minority-benefiting projects. It is whether the voters' ignorance of what is in the budget will cause governments to increase or decrease the number of such projects, thereby increasing or decreasing the budget as a whole.

As we have shown, when preponderant ignorance prevails, voters are most likely to be aware of those government policies which directly affect their sources of income. Hence they encourage government policies which raise the relative prices of the products they sell. But since any particular type of producer is in a minority in a complex society, these policies will be minority-benefiting policies. This is also true because such policies injure all buyers of the product, and buyers usually outnumber producers. Thus each citizen's perception threshold is most likely to be crossed by minority-benefiting policies involving government spending that raise (or could raise) his income.

On the other hand, government policies that affect the prices of individual goods he consumes will not be as apparent or as significant to him as policies which affect the price of what he produces. But policies that raise his costs as a consumer also benefit the citizens who produce what he consumes. It therefore appears that government can engage in specialized spending that benefits each type of producer without arousing the antagonism of consumers, especially since each consumer receives such benefits himself in his role as a producer. This situation tends to make the actual budget larger than the "correct" one.

However, this appearance is deceptive, for it ignores the cost side of the budget. When voters are preponderantly ignorant about the budget, they do not realize that special benefits are being provided to minorities to which they do not belong. But these benefits raise the general level of taxation, and voters are quite aware of their taxes, since taxes affect them directly. Thus their knowledge of the budget is narrowed down to two major items: government policies directly affecting their sources of income, and those types of taxes which inherently call themselves to every citizen's attention (e.g., income taxes).

As noted, when any minority gets special benefits from government spending, the minority's taxes are likely to go up much more than just its share of the cost of the benefits it receives. If the taxes that rise cannot be concealed from the citizenry, each minority may prefer to eschew its special benefits and vote for a budget which cuts out such benefits and reduces everyone's taxes. But if the taxes that rise are the type that are less likely to cross the citizens' perception threshold (e.g., sales taxes), then each minority may vote for a budget which provides it with special benefits because its taxes do not appear to go up significantly.

Thus, insofar as taxation can be concealed from the electorate, the government budget will tend to be larger than the "correct" one. Voters will underestimate the costs they are paying for special benefits received, and parties will build this bias into their budgets. However, this tendency does not eliminate the previously discussed tendency toward a too-small budget. Under preponderant ignorance, both forces act simultaneously; so the net outcome in terms of total budget size is ambiguous.

VIII. The Net Results

Nevertheless, I believe the actual budget will still be smaller than the "correct" budget because even indirect taxation is much more apparent than many remote government benefits. As noted previously, whoever collects indirect taxes is aware of their existence even if in the long run he does not bear them himself. He tends to look at them as expropriation by the government of resources he could collect himself, since by raising the price of his product, they reduce his sales and cause him short-run hardships. Furthermore, he attempts to placate his customers for his higher price by identifying that element of it caused by the tax— thus making them aware of it. And if this tax is significant enough to support substantial increases over the "correct" budget, it must irritate many such persons. For these reasons, it is difficult to increase taxation to support "hidden" special projects without arousing opposition. True, policies like tariffs, which raise prices but do not increase taxes, can be used to provide minorities with hidden benefits, especially if the persons whose income-earning suffers are foreign citizens. But when a domestic appropriation of revenues is necessary to support a hidden subsidy, some voters are bound to complain. This fact necessarily limits the tendency for budgets to exceed the "correct" amount.

No such inherent brake limits the tendency for remote government benefits to be ignored. Since most remote benefits stem from preventive action, no one feels any immediate loss when they are not forthcoming. Perhaps particular producers might increase their incomes if government adopted policies that produced remote benefits, but their voices are not as loud as those of the taxpayers injured by indirect taxes. In the first place, they are not suffering "expropriation" of actual private earnings but only loss of potential income, which is rationally less significant because it must be discounted for uncertainty. Second, they are usually few compared with the large number of voters who must be taxed if the budget is to be made larger than the "correct" size. Furthermore, the benefits of preventive action in any field are usually known only to experts in that field, since such knowledge implies the ability to predict future events, which in turn demands familiarity with causal relations in the field. Whenever these experts are members of the government, they are primarily motivated to produce votes rather than benefits. But remote benefits cannot produce votes unless resources are spent to inform people about them—and voters are notoriously hard to inform about anything remote. Thus the experts who usually know most about such remote benefits are not strongly motivated to produce them—nor is anyone else.

For these reasons, the two opposite tendencies acting on the budget are not of equal strength. The forces which tend to enlarge budgets beyond the "correct" level are inherently limited, whereas those which tend to shrink it are not. Therefore I believe the budget will emerge smaller than its "correct" size.

Even if the net size of the actual budget in relation to its "correct" size is ambiguous, certain specific distortions in it (i.e., variations from the "correct" budget) can be expected to result from the two tendencies described. They are as follows:

(1) Indirect taxes will be too large in relation to direct taxes.

Corollary A: Governments which depend on direct taxation for the bulk of their financing will find it more difficult to balance their budgets than similar governments which depend upon indirect financing.

Corollary B: Since the costs of inflationary finance are not as apparent as those of taxation, this method will be too frequently used to avoid increasing direct taxation.

(2) Projects which benefit minorities will be awarded too large a share of the resources allocated to government.[15]

Corollary A: Costs of projects benefiting all citizens will be distributed with too many loopholes allowing specific minorities to evade their "normal" share.

Corollary B: Producers as a group will receive a disproportionate share of government spending and policy-protection in comparison with consumers.

(3) In comparison with policies producing immediate and tangible benefits, government policies which produce remote or problematical benefits will not be allocated as many resources as are warranted by their true importance.

---

[15] This conclusion and many of the ideas in Section VII were developed in discussion with Gordon Tullock, to whom I am much indebted.

All of these tendencies distort the budget that would prevail if people were perfectly informed. Yet being perfectly informed is impossible, and even being well-informed is irrational; hence ignorance is likely to prevail. Therefore these distortions will probably occur even though a majority would be better off if they were eliminated.

IX. The Increasing Importance of the Problem

As society grows more complex, the role of governmental action becomes relatively more significant. This conclusion applies to all levels of government—local, county, state, national, and international. It results from government's function as a preventer and settler of conflicts among men.[16] Increased social complexity means increased interdependence, which in turn creates more conflicts of interest. Hence the need for more and more regulation, control, and intervention by government in all spheres of action, especially economic.

Social complexity is usually the result of an increasingly specialized division of labor, which also causes higher productivity. Thus societies tend to become richer as they grow more complex. In democracies, this increased wealth is usually distributed to all citizens—by no means equally, but in a generally rising living standard. As men become wealthier, their marginal economic desires shift from material necessities to luxuries and services. Freed from the need to direct all resources to private necessities, they can afford many collective benefits heretofore beyond their means. Thus the need for greater government action coincides with greater ability to pay for it.

However, ability to pay and desire to pay are not identical. We have shown that, in our model economic world, the citizens of a democracy are reluctant to yield their private resources to the government if the benefits to be gained thereby are at all remote from their everyday knowledge. This reluctance is not based on stupidity or irrationality, but on the ignorance in which the average citizen of a complex society is forced to live. He simply cannot afford to be well-informed about all the remote benefits of government action that are or might be important to him. And this ignorance influences the government to refrain from providing him with such benefits. The party in power fears losing to its opponents if it invests tangible resources in less tangible projects, even when it realizes that those projects would benefit the citizenry.

Furthermore, as society grows more complex, the remoteness of possible government action increases. This tendency is most obvious in

[16] This is not the sole function of government, but it is one of the most central.

international affairs, where economic and technical progress have spread a web of interdependency over the whole world. It becomes harder and harder for even experts to keep well-informed on possible benefits to be gained from government policies, including those on the local scene. In short, society's complexity demands more government action, but it also makes each field of action more remote from the ken of the average man. Faced with a gigantic maze of government agencies, each grappling with incredibly intricate problems, a normal citizen soon concludes that keeping himself well-informed is hopeless. Therefore he wraps himself in a mantle of rational ignorance, insulated from knowledge of increasingly important remote benefits by the increasingly high cost of finding out about them.

Thus, as remote benefits become more important, they become less likely to be attained. Their greater importance is accompanied by still greater remoteness, and this makes governments more wary of devoting resources to them for fear of competition from opponents who advocate more immediate gains.[17] The actual government budget shrinks to an ever-smaller percentage of the "correct" budget, even if it increases in size absolutely. Yet most people do not realize this increasing distortion because they are blanketed by an ignorance of political realities which becomes deeper and deeper as the realities become more significant. This ignorance is abetted by every citizen's belief that the government budget is too large in relation to the benefits he is getting from it, because so much of it benefits others at his expense.

CONCLUSION

In a democracy, information costs tend to make governments enact budgets that are smaller than they would be if such costs were absent. This conclusion is true even if both parties and citizens are rational in

[17] During periods of rising national income, government receipts will increase without any change in tax rates. Assuming that such increases are not accompanied by an inflation which destroys their real value, the government will have greater purchasing power available to it. It might therefore appear that government could increase its spending beyond the "correct" amount without the voters knowing about it. However, this argument ignores two facts. First, the opposition party serves as a "watchdog" ready to call voters' attention to such tendencies. If the governing party tried to increase spending covertly with these funds, the opposition might defeat it by uncovering the added receipts and promising to return them to voters via tax cuts. Second, voters will realize that their absolute taxes are rising, even if their incomes are also rising. For both reasons, voters will be aware of rising government receipts. Since the governing party has no vested interest in maximizing its spending anyway, it cannot afford to risk antagonizing voters by trying to hide such increments. Hence it will evaluate them by weighing votes, as with any other receipts, and either return them to voters via tax cuts or spend them so as to gain further support. Thus whether the model is conceived of as static or dynamic is irrelevant to its major conclusions.

their political behavior. It is based on the economic theory of democracy, which treats political parties as part of the division of labor, motivated primarily by self-interest like all other agents in the economy.

Furthermore, if economic growth is injected into the analysis, the tendency for actual budgets to be smaller than "correct" budgets becomes more and more pronounced. As society becomes more complex because of increasing specialization, the governing party is less able to allocate resources to those remote benefits which are of increasing importance to the welfare of the citizenry. It is even conceivable that the growing gap between the actual and the "correct" budgets might precipitate a crisis for democratic government. If the society were suddenly confronted by an external threat heretofore latent, its chronic tendency to underinvest in remote benefits might prove extremely deleterious, if not fatal.

However, such projection goes beyond the limits of my model. I have merely tried to use the economic theory of democracy to draw significant conclusions about democratic governments. This theory has been criticized because it cannot predict the actions of individual men, who play a central role in political events but do not always act selfishly. Therefore, it is said, the theory is useless for political analysis. But if it can reveal underlying tendencies in democracy which operate independently of individuals, then I believe it is a useful theory. In my opinion, it can be used to reach significant, non-obvious conclusions applicable to the real world—especially to the American government. I hope the analysis presented in this article provides an example of such application.

IN DEFENSE OF MAJORITY VOTING

ANTHONY DOWNS

University of Chicago

IN A recent article entitled "Problems of Majority Voting," Gordon Tullock presented an ingenious model to illustrate certain problems which he believes arise from the use of simple majority voting in democracies.[1] It is my contention that the problems he describes are not caused by majority voting and that the generalizations he makes about the real world based on the model are not true, because real democracies do not use the form of voting he sets forth. Therefore, in this article I shall attempt to defend majority voting from Tullock's attacks, though this defense does not constitute a general rationalization of majority rule.

The basic premise behind simple majority rule is that every voter should have equal weight with every other voter. Hence, if disagreement occurs, it is better for more voters to tell fewer what to do than vice versa. The only practical arrangement to accomplish this is simple majority rule. Any rule requiring more than a simple majority for passage of an act allows a minority to prevent action by the majority, thus giving the vote of each member of the minority more weight than the vote of each member of the majority. For example, if a majority of two-thirds is required for passage, then opposition by 34 per cent of the voters can prevent the other 66 per cent from carrying out their desires. In effect, the opinion of each member of the 34 per cent minority is weighted the same as the opinion of 1.94

members of the 66 per cent majority. All rules of voting other than the majority rule have this same defect.

However, as Tullock points out, the equal weighting of all votes can lead to undesirable results when voters do not have equally intense preferences. If a minority passionately desires some act which the majority just barely opposes, there is no way for the minority to express its great intensity in a simple once-for-all vote, unless buying and selling of votes is allowed. However, when a series of issues is under consideration, expression of intensities can be allowed for by the trading of votes and promises of reciprocal support among voters. It is this possibility of "logrolling" to which Tullock devotes his model.

In the model, one hundred farmers living on different roads are seeking to keep their roads repaired. Each road-repair action requires a separate vote by all the farmers, and the costs of each repair are spread evenly over all of them. If no vote-trading is allowed, every road-repair proposal will be defeated, since ninety-nine farmers will gain nothing from it but have to bear some of the costs.[2] But, if farmers are allowed to trade promises of support, then each will seek to

[1] "Problems of Majority Voting," *Journal of Political Economy*, LXVII (December, 1959), 571–79. Throughout this article the term "majority" is equivalent to "simple majority" unless otherwise stated. Both these terms refer to the nearest whole number of voters over 50 per cent of those voting in any election under consideration. I am grateful to Professor Tullock for reading the first draft of this criticism; his comments have resulted in the elimination of several errors from the final version.

[2] In some American communities—particularly in California—voters do vote directly on a large number of specific proposals for expenditure. However, few of these proposals are of the type exemplified by Tullock's model, in which expenditures benefit individual voters directly. Most of the proposals which voters pass upon benefit very few voters directly, except for occasional neighborhood-improvement effects. Spending on such projects as jails, mental hospitals, and other state institutions must, for most voters, be judged on the basis of whether the benefits to the *community as a whole* justify additional tax burdens which they *personally* will bear. This involves a different kind of judgment from that discussed by Tullock. Thus, even though too many citizens vote to make logrolling possible, such expenditure bills are often passed.

enter into agreements with at least fifty others so that he can insure that his road will be repaired in return for his supporting repair of their roads.

Remarkably enough, the result of this process is that every farmer finds himself paying more in taxes for the repairs of other roads than he gets for the repair of his own. He is financially a net loser from government action—but so is every other farmer. Hence the farmers as a group behave irrationally because they devote too many resources to repairing their roads; yet it is individually rational for them to do so.

Tullock reaches this conclusion via the following reasoning. In order to get his own road-repair bill passed, each farmer must obtain the support of fifty others, which he does by agreeing to support the road-repair bills of each of them. The amount of resources devoted to repairs in each such bill is arrived at by balancing the marginal cost against the marginal benefit. That is, each farmer weighs the amount he will receive when his own bill is passed against the total cost to him of supporting his bill and the fifty others. However, this cost is borne not only by the fifty-one farmers in the bargain but also by the forty-nine other farmers not in the bargain. Thus, he stands to gain about $\frac{1}{51}$ of the total cost for a payment of only $\frac{1}{100}$ of it. Assuming diminishing marginal utility of income and of road repairs, this means he is willing to request for himself—and support for others—a higher level of road repair than he would if he had to pay $\frac{1}{51}$ of the cost. He raises the level of road repair he is willing to support until he is in marginal equilibrium between gains from road repair and losses from taxes.

However, his calculation turns out to be in error. This occurs because the fifty farmers he has bargained with are also in similar bargains—but not all with each other. Instead, many of them have included in their bargains some of the forty-nine farmers not in his bargain and excluded some of the fifty in his bargain. A system of "revolving majorities" has sprung up because the forty-nine farmers who were left out when

the first set of bills was passed have successfully offered excellent "deals" to some members of the majority bloc, wooing these members into supporting their bills too. Thus, as many as one hundred road-repair bills will in fact be passed, although nearly every farmer individually is making calculations as though only the fifty-one bills he is supporting will be passed. Since he will have to pay $\frac{1}{100}$ of all one hundred bills (assuming one hundred are passed), he comes out paying much more than he calculated, and he finds himself out of balance at the margin.

It might be argued that he will learn from this experience and lower the level of repair he will support, because he will guess that he will be forced to pay for one hundred bills instead of just fifty-one. But he will always seek to maximize the amount spent in his own repair bill, since the more he gets, the more likely he is to offset the unknown costs that will fall on him from others. Similarly, the other fifty men in his bargain are all seeking to maximize their own bills. If any one of them refuses to go along with the others, they will not support his high level of repairs. Thus, he is forced into continuing his support of large repairs, even though they make him a net loser. Only if he can create a permanent cartel out of fifty-one farmers can a lower level be enforced. However, in that case there is no reason to have lower levels, since the cartel can defeat all forty-nine other road-repair bills. But such cartels cannot hang together because the forty-nine non-members can make such an outstanding offer to any two members of the cartel that they cannot rationally resist it. Thus no fifty-one-farmer combination can dominate all others; so revolving majorities spring up, and overinvestment in road repairs inevitably results.

From this ingenious model Tullock expands to the following general conclusions:

1. Government activity which benefits minorities will receive disproportionate allocations of resources in comparison with that which benefits the citizenry as a whole.

2. Taxes of general impact will be riddled

with exemptions favoring special groups.

3. The government budget as a whole will be too large, because each citizen will be driven by individual rationality to support a level of government spending which is irrational as a whole.

This makes almost every citizen a net financial loser to the government sector. Tullock believes these conclusions are applicable to the real world as well as his model. He states that the undesirable conditions they portray arise "from the system of compelling the minority to accept the will of the majority."

It is my contention that these conditions —even if they exist in the real world—are not the result of the majority principle at all. In order to prove this point, I must first examine the assumptions which underlie Tullock's model. The model is based upon the following premises:

1. Acts of legislation can discriminate between individuals regarding expenditures but not regarding taxation. That is, every tax must be levied upon all equally, but spending can be directed toward particular individuals only. This we shall call the *discrimination* assumption.

2. Acts of legislation are voted upon directly by the citizenry. This we shall call the *referendum* assumption.

3. The road-repair program is never considered as a whole but is broken into individual projects which are put to a vote one at a time. Thus, the voters face a continuing series of proposals spread over time, and the outcome of future votes is never known at the time of each present vote. We shall call this the *seriatim* assumption.

4. Voters can effectively bargain with each other and make viable promises of vote-trading. Following Tullock, we shall label this the *logrolling* assumption.

5. Each act proposed for a vote is carried if a majority supports it. This is the *majority* assumption.

6. A fairly large number of acts can be proposed and will actually be put to a vote. This we shall call the *multiple-activity* assumption.

7. Voting occurs on one and only one issue— road-repairing. We shall call this the *exclusiveness* assumption. (Tullock specifically relaxes

this assumption before making his general conclusions.)

Once we have spelled out these assumptions, it is apparent that most of them are not applicable to real-world democracies and that the majority assumption is not the cause of the results of Tullock's model. Let us examine these two contentions in order.

Of the seven assumptions upon which Tullock's model is based, only two—the discrimination and majority assumptions—are actually operative in most real-world democracies.[3] Since most democratic societies use republican forms of government, the other assumptions simply do not apply. Citizens do not vote directly upon individual legislative acts; they do not vote on a continuing series of proposals but face periodic elections in which the government's entire program is considered as a whole; they do not bargain directly with each other; they cannot consider a large number of proposals in a given time period; and, when they do vote, their vote covers a multitude of issues all at once.[4]

These objections might be countered by the argument that the assumptions which are not true of the real world do not have any bearing on Tullock's conclusions anyway. However, this is false. In particular, the seriatim assumption is the main pillar of his reasoning. If voters consider the entire road program as a whole every so often, instead of voting on individual road-

[3] The discrimination assumption is not operative in cases where taxes are aimed at specific groups, such as a special assessment to pay for a local street.

[4] In some cases citizens do vote directly upon individual legislative acts, as described in n. 2. However, even in these cases the acts voted upon comprise only a small fraction of all the acts considered by the legislature, and citizens cannot bargain directly with each other because the number of voters is too large. Thus Tullock's model—which is based upon personal bargaining and vote-trading among individual voters—does not accurately describe even those few parts of the world in which direct referendums play a significant role in expenditure decision-making.

repair proposals one at a time, their "collective irrationality" disappears. To prove this, let us propose another model in which political parties exist, motivated by the desire to be elected. Each party formulates an over-all road program which it presents to the voters in competition with the programs presented by other parties. The party getting the most votes is allowed to carry out its proposals. Clearly, no voter will support a program which requires him to pay more in taxes than he receives in benefits if a better alternative is available. Hence, no party will formulate a program which requires a majority to do this. It is true that a majority bloc might form and vote roads only for itself, paid for both by itself and by the minority who got no roads. (Tullock also mentions this possibility but rules it out because of his seriatim assumption.) Thus, a minority might find itself sustaining net losses through government action. But this conclusion is vastly different from Tullock's argument that all citizens (or at least a substantial majority) would be net losers. Since the majority would be net gainers, we could not conclude that the government budget was too large. It is clear that the whole burden of Tullock's argument rests upon the voters considering each road repair bill as an isolated act, separate from other such bills, rather than considering all repairs at once as part of a unified program. This fact remains true whether acts are passed by a majority or by some fraction larger than a majority. Thus, Tullock's major conclusion results from the seriatim assumption, not the majority assumption.

In the real world the seriatim assumption is not valid. Voters elect representatives who pass upon individual acts in a legislature. However, each representative knows that he must face his constituents at the end of the election period with the net result of all his individual legislative behavior. If he has supported such a high level of road repairs that all his constituents are paying out more than the benefits they receive, he is sure to be defeated by an opponent who

promises to reduce the level of repairs and the over-all tax bill so that they balance each other. Thus, the fact that he knows the voters will consider his performance as a whole forces him to prevent the majority of his constituents from winding up net losers from government action. His survival in office is at stake, and politicians place a high value upon survival in office.

Nevertheless, it could be argued that the legislator is faced with the same problem in the assembly that the farmers are in Tullock's model. In the real world, within the legislature itself the first six assumptions behind Tullock's reasoning are all applicable. Only the exclusiveness assumption does not hold true. If we set it aside for the moment, would not each legislator be driven by individual rationality to creating a program for his constituency containing the same over-all imbalance that plagues the farmers in Tullock's model?

To explore this possibility further, we shall borrow a model from an unpublished study by Tullock which analyzes the behavior of a legislature.[5] Assume that there are one hundred districts, each composed exactly like the farm community in Tullock's published model. Each district elects, by majority vote, a representative to this state legislature, which decides what road repairs will be made. The legislature considers road-repair programs for individual districts one at a time, and each program which receives the support of a majority passes. The cost of all programs that are passed is spread evenly over all citizens via equal taxes, regardless of the benefits each receives. At the end of the legislative period the individual legislators return to their districts to stand for election "on their records." The citizens of each district do not vote on anything except approval or disapproval of the legislator who has served them—there are no referendums between

[5] Gordon Tullock, *A Preliminary Investigation of the Theory of Constitutions* (Department of International Studies, University of South Carolina, 1959). (Mimeographed.)

general elections. Nor are there any other issues before the legislature except the repair of roads.

If successful voting blocs could be formed under these circumstances, then a minority of 26 per cent of the citizens might exploit all the rest, as Tullock points out in his manuscript. In each district fifty-one farmers could form a solid electoral bloc and elect a representative who would act in their interest only. Then in the legislature fifty-one of these representatives could form a parliamentary bloc which would approve a high level of road repairs for the majority in each of their own districts and no repairs for the minority in these districts or for anyone in the forty-nine non-bloc districts. Thus, 26 per cent of the voters would have very well-repaired roads, and 74 per cent would have no repairs at all, though the costs were spread over all of them. This startling exploitation of a majority by a minority appears to be the final result of using majority rule![6]

However, the voting blocs formed in this way would not be stable. The forty-nine legislators whose constituents were paying taxes but getting no repairs would face certain defeat in their home districts by electoral opponents who would promise to do better. To avoid this catastrophe, they would band together and offer two of the members of the majority bloc extravagantly

large road repairs in return for desertion of the old majority bloc and formation of a new one. These two legislators could not resist such an offer. If they did, they would also face electoral defeat at home by opponents who promised to take up the offer—thus providing much better roads for the voters at little added cost. Hence the old majority block would break up, and a new one would form—but it would be vulnerable to the same type of disintegration. As Tullock argues in the case of the farmers, no group of fifty-one can dominate all other groups; hence no stable majority blocs can be formed at all. Instead, myriads of individual bargains will occur, and each legislator will make "deals" with fifty others to support their road-repair bills in return for their support of his. But this will result in a series of bills passed by "revolving majorities," and each individual legislator will find himself in the same position as are the farmers in Tullock's model. He will calculate the level of repairs to support on the assumption that fifty-one repair programs will be passed but, in fact, one hundred will pass (or, at least, many more than fifty-one), and he will discover that the tax load for his district exceeds the gains the district will receive from road repairs. This irrational outcome will occur in every district. Apparently, Tullock's argument applies to legislative government as well as to government by referendum, and we can expect the government budget to be too large in both cases.

However, appearances are deceiving in political theory, because there is one factor at work in this legislative model that is not at work in the model composed of individual farmers: electoral competition. Any legislator who returns to his constituents with a record featuring more costs than benefits is sure to be defeated by an opponent promising the reverse. Thus, the fact that his district emerges from the legislative process with a net loss is not just a marginal loss of utility to him—it is politically fatal. Although each individual farmer might be prepared to absorb a net loss from road referendums as an inevitable result of the system,

[6] However, this outcome is extremely unlikely because of the secret ballot. Since no legislator can be positive who voted for him and who voted against him, he must spread the benefits of his policies over all citizens in his district who might have been responsible for getting him elected. Only if he has been supported by a personally identifiable bloc of 51 per cent of his constituents can he afford to ignore the other 49 per cent—and even in that case the need to "take out a little insurance" would probably prompt him to benefit a few more citizens just in case some members of his supporting bloc defected. Thus, even if 51 per cent of the legislators form a solid bloc in the legislature, where open voting is the rule, the benefits of their policies will be spread over many more than 26 per cent of all the voters—up to as many as 51 per cent. I am indebted to James Q. Wilson of the University of Chicago for pointing out this fact.

individual politicians cannot take the same resigned attitude toward electoral defeat.[7]

Instead, they will struggle desperately against losing their offices in one of two ways. First, they can try to reconstitute majority blocs. However, such blocs are inherently unstable, as we have shown. Therefore, this approach offers no permanent solution. Second, they can pass a law which prohibits discriminatory expenditures. Such a law would state that the same standard of road repair must be administered to all roads, just as the costs of these roads are levied against all citizens. This law would prevent any district from emerging from the legislative process with a net loss from the road program (assuming zero administrative costs and an equal number of roads in all districts). Thus, no legislator would be forced to return to his district saddled with a record of loss to his constituents. True, he also could not hope to exploit the citizens of other districts or minorities in his own district in order to "pay off" the majority which elected him. But, faced with the alternatives of non-discrimination or certain defeat, every legislator would find it in his interest to choose the former.

Thus the legislative model can have one of two outcomes: (1) chronic instability can result, with a constant attempt to create majority blocs, which soon dissolve and are replaced by others equally short-lived; or (2) laws against discriminatory spending can be passed. In neither case are Tullock's generalized conclusions valid.[8]

However, the preceding argument is intuitively unsatisfactory because, in the real world, legislatures do not seem to behave this way. On the contrary, logrolling similar to that described by Tullock appears much more realistic than either of the two

logically superior outcomes mentioned above. Are we forced, then, to conclude that Tullock's argument is indeed quite applicable to the real world?

The answer is "No." The disproof of Tullock's contentions must take place on two levels: that of a model world and that of the real world. We have already shown that, in Tullock's own model, collective irrationality is not caused by majority rule but by serial voting on a continuous stream of proposals. When the voters choose among road programs periodically on an all-and-once basis, collective irrationality disappears, regardless of whether majority rule is used. Furthermore, the kind of collective irrationality Tullock describes does not arise even if we extend the model to include a legislature. It is not true that the majority is forced into the position of paying more for government action than they get out of it. Thus, on the level of the model world, Tullock's argument that logrolling causes collective irrationality is false. *Ipso facto*, his argument that majority rule causes such irrationality via logrolling must also be false.

This leaves only two of Tullock's contentions about model worlds still standing. Of these, I accept his argument that logrolling (that is, the trading of votes) is to the advantage of its participants and therefore exists when it is legal. But I do not believe that such vote-trading is caused by use of majority rule. To prove this, let us assume

[7] If each does accept his defeat as certain, he loses all motivation for furthering the interests of his constituents. Instead he will exploit his office—while it lasts—purely for personal gain (which may take the form of pride in excellent statesmanship as well as financial prosperity). In this case the basic structure of the representative system breaks down, since the representatives have no motive for acting in the interests of those who elect them.

[8] A third outcome is possible—the one described in n. 7. This outcome is the only one consistent with Tullock's generalized conclusions, but it is self-contradictory in the long run. If elected representatives in some areas always face certain defeat when running for re-election, they will abandon their function as representatives of their constituents. In this case the constituents will not long tolerate continued operation of democracy or continued membership in this geographical grouping. Either they will agitate for a dictatorship or some other non-democratic system which gives more weight to their interests, or they will attempt to secede from that particular democracy and set up another one in which their interests will be better served. Thus, the model which supports Tullock's conclusions also implies internal conflict which will tend to destroy the political society it posits.

that no measure can pass a legislature unless it receives the support of 90 per cent of the members. In this case, if 91 per cent of the members are mildly in favor of a bill to deport all Jews to Israel (to use Tullock's example) but the other 9 per cent are violently opposed, logrolling will still occur. The minority will still seek to protect their interest on issues about which they feel very strongly by trading votes in support of issues to which they are only mildly opposed. The only situation in which no vote-trading of this type would occur is one in which unanimous consent is required for passage of a bill.[9] In that case every minority can protect itself (assuming it has at least one representative in the legislature) without bargaining to do so. But the cost of such protection in terms of equality of representation is high. If there are one hundred legislators, and ninety-nine wish to pass a bill but one opposes it, the weight accorded that one is ninety-nine times as great as the weight given each of the others on that issue.

As already pointed out, such unequal weighting of votes is inevitable in any system which requires more than a simple majority for passage of a bill. Yet every such system would also give rise to logrolling. Thus, logrolling is an inescapable result of the following conditions:

1. Two or more different issues are under consideration by an electorate (which may be a legislature).
2. The electorate is small enough to make individual bargaining and vote-trading practical.
3. Individual bargaining and vote-trading are legal.
4. Differing opinions exist among the voters about the issues under consideration.

5. Varying intensities of opinion exist about these issues.
6. The issues are voted upon separately instead of being considered all at once as a unified program.

Whenever these conditions exist simultaneously, logrolling is almost certain to occur. Thus, logrolling is not caused by majority rule but by the existence of the above conditions under any form of rule whatsoever except one-man dictatorship, in which vote-trading cannot occur because only one man votes. But only under majority rule are the preferences of each voter given equal weight in the act of choice. That is why majority rule has been so often adopted as the fairest way to make decisions when opinions differ.

Having disposed of Tullock's contentions in the model world, let us turn to his statements about the real world. Tullock's model appeared more realistic than the model we developed to refute his arguments because his model led to logrolling—which we see everywhere in the real world, whereas our model led to prevention of discriminatory spending—an outcome opposite to that we see in the real world. However, I believe this is the result of assuming that only one issue (road-repairing) exists. If many issues exist, it is not possible for a legislature to pass a law against discriminatory spending. Because the effect of each particular expenditure upon each individual citizen cannot be measured in the same way that the level of road repairs could be, it is inevitable that some bills will benefit certain persons more than others. In fact, most bills in the real world are specifically designed to benefit minority groups. This outcome is unavoidable in a highly differentiated society, where specialization creates minority groups with objective interests which differ widely from each other. Since each minority group seeks to pass certain measures that benefit it specifically, its members agree to trade votes with other minority groups seeking majority support for measures beneficial to them, and logrolling arises. Because logrolling thus occurs in the model we used to

[9] Even under unanimous rule, vote-trading would still occur. Since every individual would have power of veto over every bill, each could "blackmail" any majority which wanted to pass a bill by threatening to withdraw his vote unless some bill he wanted was also passed. The impossibility of creating 100 per cent cartels because of this constant threat of "blackmail" is what makes unanimous rule so impractical.

refute Tullock when we allow many issues to exist, this model no longer appears less realistic than Tullock's model.

However, the question then becomes whether this process leads to the kind of collective irrationality which Tullock envisages. My answer is that the outcome depends upon whether issues are considered only serially or whether at some point in the process the ultimate electorate makes an all-at-once choice between alternate *over-all* programs of action. In the real world the latter situation prevails; hence, I do not believe that logrolling causes the kind of collective irrationality which Tullock describes.

True, it might do so if certain kinds of ignorance prevail. If, for example, as Tullock mentions in his article, voters are ignorant of some of the costs imposed upon them through indirect taxation, they may vote for a program which includes a government budget that is "really" too large. This would occur because their act of balancing losses to government and gains from it at the margin would be in error, since they would not be taking into account those losses of which they were ignorant. But, if we admit ignorance into the picture, voters may also be ignorant of benefits they receive. As I argue elsewhere, the total effect of ignorance in the

real world is, in my opinion, a government budget that is too small.[10]

To sum up our analysis of Tullock's implications about the real-world meaning of his model, we may state the following:

1. Logrolling does exist in the real world, but it is just as compatible with our model as with Tullock's.

2. Logrolling is not caused specifically by simple majority rule but by any type of collective decision-making other than one-man dictatorship.

3. If collective irrationality like that described by Tullock occurs in the real world, it is not for the reasons Tullock states, because issues are not considered serially by the ultimate electorate in the real world.

4. If such collective irrationality exists in the real world, it is caused by ignorance, and it may take the form of a government budget that is too small as well as one that is too large.

Thus, majority rule is not really the villain Tullock made it out to be. The problems he described as caused by majority rule either do not really exist, are caused by ignorance, or are inherent in the process of collective decision-making, no matter what rule is employed. But only the majority principle guarantees that every vote will have the same weight as every other vote.

[10] This argument is presented in "Why the Government Budget Is Too Small in a Democracy," *World Politics*, July, 1960.

start

next page

[4]

THE PUBLIC INTEREST:
ITS MEANING IN A DEMOCRACY

BY ANTHONY DOWNS

Since its appearance, the political model in my book *An Economic Theory of Democracy* has been criticized—in this journal, among others—because it does not include any concept of the public interest.[1] The book's critics argue that a theory of political action based on economic principles and containing only self-interested actors cannot explain those crucial political decisions that are made by men acting for the common good instead of their own. In my opinion these attacks are partially justified by certain defects in my economic model of political behavior. However, I also believe that this model can be amended to eliminate its defects without any basic alteration of its nature. After such amendment the economic theory of democracy should prove a useful tool for placing the concept of public interest in its proper perspective in relation to real-world political behavior. In the following pages I shall attempt to prove these assertions.

Functions of the Concept

The term public interest is constantly used by politicians, lobbyists, political theorists, and voters, but any detailed inquiry about its exact meaning plunges the inquirer into a welter of platitudes, generalities, and philosophic arguments. It soon becomes apparent that no general agreement exists about whether the term has any meaning at all, or, if it has, what the meaning is, which specific

---

[1] For a statement of the economic theory of democracy see Anthony Downs, "An Economic Theory of Political Action in a Democracy," in *Journal of Political Economy*, vol. 65 (April 1957) pp. 135–50, and *An Economic Theory of Democracy* (New York 1957). The principal criticisms were raised by Gerhard Colm, "In Defense of the Public Interest," in *Social Research*, vol. 27 (Autumn 1960) pp. 295–307; by Martin Diamond, book review in *Journal of Political Economy*, vol. 67 (April 1959) pp. 208–11; and by A. Bergson, book review in *American Economic Review*, vol. 48 (June 1958) pp. 437–40.

actions are in the public interest and which are not, and how to distinguish between them. In the face of this confusion, why is the term so often used? The answer can be found by distinguishing between the meaning of a concept and its functions. Many a significant concept is extremely hard to define in such a way that a large number of its users would agree on the definition. One reason it is so hard to define terms like love, justice, and power is that they refer to realities so fundamental and all-pervasive in our lives that we cannot encompass them in a few words. Yet everyone who uses such a concept has a notion of what it means, and employs that notion to order the events he encounters and to communicate his thoughts to others. The concept public interest falls in this category. Nevertheless it serves important functions in social life.

To appreciate its functions, let us first postulate a society made up of individuals who have identical preferences and identical views about the proper goals in life for individuals and for society as a whole. They also are free of excessive self-interest (that is, they do not weight their own preferences more heavily than those of others), are economically organized in a highly specialized division of labor, and live in a world with a normal degree of uncertainty and costliness of information. Under such conditions there would arise a need for a government that would at least (among its other duties) provide a framework of behavior rules for all citizens and coordinate those individual actions that could not be efficiently handled through decentralized decision-making processes like markets. The officials in such a government would make decisions by considering the good of society as a whole. Thus the public interest would consist of those government actions that most benefited the whole society. This is the basic definition that will be used throughout this paper.

In this imaginary society, where the values of the whole would not differ from those of any specific individuals, the public interest would have easily specifiable substantive content, and both the function and the motive of all government officials would be to

make decisions in the public interest.   Such a society would be in
effect a single entity, and the functions of its parts would be defined
in terms of the goals or purpose of the whole.   In real life, individuals do not have identical preferences or identical personal and
social goals, and are not free of excessive self-interest.   Realistically, therefore, society cannot be regarded as a single entity.
Nevertheless, social scientists as well as other citizens are often
forced to conceive of society as a unit, in order to understand and
discuss certain relationships between its parts.

In a democracy each citizen, in order to pass judgment on the
performance of his government, whether he does so as voter or as
lobbyist, must at least implicitly view its actions in relation to its
proper function as he defines it.   In this paper I assume that all
citizens who adhere to a democratic system agree that the proper
function of government is to act for the greatest benefit of society
as a whole, even though they may disagree widely about what
actions are best for it in any given circumstances.   (In view of the
democratic premise that all men are politically and legally of equal
"ultimate" value, even those citizens who believe the government
should act only for the greatest benefit of some particular individual, group, or class rarely advocate such a policy explicitly as
the proper function of a democratic government.)   Therefore, in
judging government performance, each citizen tacitly assumes that
society is a unit and has a single set of values that can be projected into the detailed determination of policy.   The specific
policies derived from this single set of values constitute the public
interest as viewed by that particular citizen.   In other words, *his*
view of the public interest is represented by whatever policies he
believes the government ought to carry out.   Because no two
people are identical, each citizen is likely to differ from the other
in the set of goals he imputes to the government.   Nevertheless,
everyone implicitly regards some set of goals as proper to the
government, and defines the public interest in terms of those goals.
This explains why everyone talks about the public interest, but
few agree fully about the particular policies it comprises.

Viewed in this manner, the concept of public interest has three specific functions in a democratic society (we are here concerned only with its application to government actions, even though actions of private citizens, companies, or groups may also be judged as to whether they are "in the public interest"). First, it serves as a device by which individual citizens can judge government actions and communicate their judgments to one another. Second, since the concept implies that there is one common good for all members of society, transcending the good of any one member, appeals to the public interest can be used to coopt or to placate persons who are required by government policy to act against their own immediate interests. Third, the concept serves as a guide to and a check on public officials who are faced with decisions regarding public policy but have no unequivocal instructions from the electorate or their superiors regarding what action to take.

As regards this last function, there are many rules that the officials could conceivably adopt in such circumstances—for example, maximizing the chances that their party will be reelected. But no matter what rule they in fact use, they must be able to defend each decision on the ground that it is "in the public interest." This is true because each citizen judges the performance of government on the assumption that its function is to further the welfare of the whole society as he defines that welfare (selfishly or not). The official's defense must normally include showing a logical relationship between his decision and *his* definition of society's welfare. If the official's definition is sufficiently close to the definition of those challenging him, and if he can show a reasonable relationship between his decision and that definition, he can presumably satisfy their questions, even if his actual motive for making the particular decision had nothing whatever to do with the welfare of society as a whole. The necessity of defending himself in this manner checks each public official from totally disregarding the welfare of potential questioners. It also forces him to develop a concrete concept of the public interest which may serve him as a guide when other rules are not sufficient to determine the best action at a given moment.

It is worth noting again that these functions can be carried out regardless of whether the concept of public interest can be substantively defined in any way that would be agreed on by any large number of persons. Since the concept is extremely useful in public life even though there may be almost no agreement about what it means, we can expect it to remain a permanent part of the democratic political scene.

The concept of public interest is closely related to the minimal consensus necessary for the operation of a democratic society. This consists of an implicit agreement among the preponderance of the people concerning two main areas: the basic rules of conduct and decision-making that should be followed in the society; and general principles regarding the fundamental social policies that the government ought to carry out. Because the minimal consensus is so crucial in both political theory and the actual operation of societies, it is worth closer examination.

Every society operates by means of basic behavior rules that its members are supposed to follow. Such rules are necessary so that each person can predict the reactions of others to social situations with enough accuracy that normal interaction can occur without undue uncertainty and anxiety. The fact that not everyone always follows these rules does not invalidate their fundamental importance. Although the rules are ultimately derived from ethical values, in a democratic society the consensus usually concerns the rules themselves rather than the values underlying them. This is true because the same rule may be derived from several different ultimate values, and in a pluralistic society there is often considerable disagreement concerning ultimate values. Since the proponents of these differing values must live together they agree on certain behavior rules, which then become intermediate values in themselves.[2]

---

[2] Jacques Maritain presents a cogent statement of this view in his *The Range of Reason* (New York 1952) pp. 165–71.

Among the types of rules that form part of this minimal consensus are those of personal conduct and those of political conduct. The first are derived from the general code of morality professed by most members of the society. In Western nations such rules are historically related to religious values like the Ten Commandments and the Golden Rule. This category also includes those rules that natural-law theorists would argue are apprehensible through natural reason. Rules of political conduct derive from the written or traditional constitution. Many attempts have been made to specify the minimum political rules necessary for democracy, but here I mention only two as examples. First, when the incumbent party is defeated in a legitimate election, it must relinquish office peacefully to the victors. Second, in some ultimate sense men are of equal value; therefore each citizen's preferences should receive the same ethical weighting as each other citizen's, and it is better for a majority to impose decisions on a minority than vice versa.

It should be pointed out that these rules are almost never written down together and identified as the minimal consensus, nor are they consciously and explicitly agreed to by a majority or even a sizable number of the members of society. Rather they are part of the basic culture that is passed on from generation to generation and constantly reinforced through schools, family life, churches, and other institutions engaged in enculturation and social control. In essence these rules constitute a "social contract," analogous to that which classical political theorists assumed to be at the root of each society, although this "contract" is only implicitly "signed" by each person as he absorbs its values in the process of growing up and living in the society.

Another part of the minimal consensus consists of a vague image of "the good society." This can be viewed as the type of polity that would exist if the behavior rules in the consensus were put into action, but it goes farther and includes certain policy principles—for example, "the government ought to do something to prevent serious depressions." At a given time it may not be clear just which principles are part of this consensus and which are simply widespread views, since the prevailing image of the good society changes considerably over long spans of time. Nevertheless, there must be preponderant agreement about the basic nature of social policy in a democracy if it is to function peacefully. Without such agreement the society cannot cope with its long-run problems, either because it cannot maintain sufficient stability of policy or because its policies are too indecisive. If the views of the citizenry are polarized into two or more extreme positions involving mutually exclusive policies, the electoral defeat of an incumbent party representing one extreme by an opposition party representing another will cause such a radical switch in government policy that civil war may occur. On the other hand, if no party can get a majority and a coalition has to govern, the coalition may be so paralyzed by its inability to obtain agreement on any one decisive policy that the problems it faces will get out of control. In either case the future of democracy is dim (postwar France offers an example of both these situations).

The above observations reveal certain important characteristics of the minimal consensus. In the first place, although some of the personal-conduct rules and political principles in it can be described specifically, much of its content consists of policy principles statable only in a vague and generalized form. Second, over the long run its content changes as new rules or policies become almost universally accepted and others are gradually abandoned. Third, even though a great many people may agree on general principles, there is almost sure to be a wide variety of views concerning how to apply those principles to concrete situations. Since many decisions that affect society in general—and therefore lie within the realm of the public interest—concern choices among extremely detailed policy alternatives, the minimal consensus underlying democracy cannot be used as a guide in making such decisions, except in a very general way.

One central aspect of the minimal consensus must be explored further in order to clarify a fundamental question about the public interest. Essentially, the consensus embodies part of the basic value structure of a democratic society. If such a society is to be meaningfully differentiated from one that is not democratic, it must include certain "absolute" values within its consensus—certain types of behavior and of relationships between the rulers and the ruled not present in non-democratic societies. Admittedly, it is very difficult to pinpoint these attributes exactly, but if they are missing from a society's minimal consensus, it is not a democratic society (for present purposes it is irrelevant whether societies should be democratic, and whether there are certain social conditions in which democracy cannot function effectively or its normal procedures must be temporarily suspended). These indispensable "absolute" values are most likely to lie in that portion of the consensus concerning rules of individual conduct and political behavior, rather than in the portion concerning desired social policies.

Let us consider now the relationship between the minimal consensus and the public interest. It is clear that in any society a government policy cannot be in the public interest if it contradicts the elements of the minimal value structure that define the society as such. Thus in a democratic society no policy can be in the public interest if it violates that portion of the minimal consensus concerning the proper rules of conduct and political behavior in that society; if it did, it would threaten the basis of democracy. Of course, in any social system there are some who favor a different system, but theirs may be said to be "system-changing" concepts of the public interest, in contrast to "intra-system" concepts. In a democracy anyone who desires the continuance of a democratic society, and therefore participates in the minimal consensus concerning rules of individual and political behavior, must have an intra-system concept of the public interest, even if he advocates change in specific social policies (for example, a person can favor abandoning social security without really seeking to alter the

basically democratic nature of the society).   In this article I
address myself only to the intra-system public interest in a democracy, unless otherwise noted.

With this definition in mind we can now deduce the following
principle: anything that is in the long run detrimental to the
majority of citizens cannot be in the public interest, unless it is
essential to the protection of those individual rights included
in the minimal consensus.   This principle of long-run majority
benefit follows from the principle of majority rule, which is in
turn derived from the axiom that each man has an "ultimate"
value equal to that of each other man.   The principle of long-
run majority benefit also provides the basic link in a democratic
society between the public interest and the private interests of the
citizenry.   Some of its further implications will be discussed later.

The personal commitment to the continuance of the rules
specified in the minimal consensus implies that each citizen is
willing to sacrifice his own short-run interests to at least some
extent if those interests require behavior or policies detrimental
to the survival of democracy; in other words, he has a positive
desire for the survival of the system.   His commitment is not
necessarily based on altruism; it can be simply an expression of
long-run self-interest.   But it must be widespread if the system
is to survive both external and internal threats to its existence.
In this respect democracy differs from totalitarian systems, which
can survive even if the vast majority of their members oppose
them.   Moreover, the destruction of democracy by its members'
excessive concentration on short-run self-interest can occur even
when they do not prefer any other political system and would
actually choose democracy over all other systems if faced with an
explicit choice.

The preceding analysis provides the basis for several conclusions,
which may be stated in summary form.   1) In a pluralistic society
there are many different views about the ultimate values proper
to individuals and society; hence it is not necessarily possible to
obtain widespread consensus about these values.   2) Nevertheless,

a preponderant majority of citizens agree on the basic social rules necessary for operation of a democracy. For the most part such agreement, represented by the minimal consensus, is necessarily rather generalized and vague, but it does contain certain specific "absolute" principles without which the democracy cannot exist. 3) Every citizen in a democracy has at least an implicit conception of the public interest, that is, a more or less detailed specification of how the government ought to carry out its function in society. 4) Since citizens differ widely in values and characteristics, there is a wide variety of conceptions of what the public interest consists of. 5) Each person may believe his conception superior to all others, but it is not possible for any citizen or government official to derive a single view that can be considered the one and only best conception of the public interest, because for this the ultimate values of the citizenry are too diverse, and the minimal consensus is too vague and imprecise. 6) Nevertheless, the political competition for office forces each public official or politician to develop some conception of the public interest by which he can, on demand, defend his particular official decisions. From the citizens' point of view, his function is to make decisions in the public interest, and therefore it is rational for them to require him to be able to defend his actions on that ground, even if they were in fact made by some other criterion. From the official's point of view, developing a public-interest conception and linking it to his decisions in a plausible manner is, at the very least, part of his struggle to stay in office through the support of a majority of voters; and in some cases the existence of such a conception may guide him in making decisions he could not reach by means of any other rule (such as winning office).

Content of the Public Interest

Up to now our discussion has focused mainly on the functions of the public-interest concept. But most of the controversy about the public interest concerns its specific substantive content—or at least how one goes about discovering its content. Here my approach makes use of the extensive analysis set forth by Glendon Schubert, whose book on the subject is devoted entirely to this problem.[3]

According to Schubert there are three major schools of thought on this subject, whose views can be briefly summarized as follows. First, the rationalist school believes that the public interest consists of "the will of the people," that is, what the government ought to do is what the people want it to do. Therefore the task of government officials is strictly a technical one: they should find out what the people want and then do it. The term "the people" is rarely defined, but it refers to at least a majority of citizens.

Second, the idealist school believes that the public interest consists of the course of action that is best for society as a whole according to some absolute standard of values, regardless of whether any citizens actually desire this course of action. Therefore the task of government officials is to be fully acquainted with that standard of values and to apply it to concrete situations by means of their own judgment. Public opinion need not be consulted, though it should be educated to understand the wisdom of the policies arrived at.

Third, the realist school believes that the public interest has no definable content per se, but that the term "in the public interest" can be applied to the results of certain *methods* of decision-making. This school in turn has three major branches. The "Bentleyan realists" contend, as Schubert puts it (p. 202), that "the public interest has significance only as the slogan which symbolizes the compromise resulting from a particular accommodation or adjustment of group interaction." In other words, the public interest has no ethical implications; it is merely whatever policies emerge from the struggle among pressure groups, no matter what decision-making method created them. The "psychological realists," on the other hand, believe that public officials are stimulated by the

[3] Glendon Schubert, *The Public Interest* (Glencoe, Illinois, 1960). I do not agree with Schubert's selection and use of the terms rationalist, idealist, and realist, but I accept them here for convenience.

concept of public interest to take some account of the welfare of citizens not directly represented by pressure groups. Thus for them the concept has the "hair-shirt" function of modifying the pressure-group struggle somewhat, through the value systems of public officials. Finally, the "due-process realists" think that decisions are in the public interest if the method of making them allows all those who might be affected to have some voice in their formation. People will accept democratic decision-making as long as they feel they have a chance to influence policy in their own favor, even if they are not always successful in doing so. Therefore we ought to use such methods, because they maximize acceptance of the resulting decisions, and "the job of official decision-makers . . . is to maximize continuity and stability in public policy; or, in other words, to minimize disruption in existing patterns of accommodation among affected interests" (p. 204).

Schubert himself rejects all of these concepts as non-operational, and concludes that "political scientists might better spend their time nurturing concepts that offer greater promise of becoming useful tools in the scientific study of political responsibility" (p. 224). However, each of these schools has in my opinion some partial truth to contribute to our understanding of the public interest; therefore it is worth while to discuss each briefly.

While public opinion certainly has some role in government decision-making, the rationalist school places too much stress on that role. There are several reasons why government officials cannot in reality be guided by the "will of the people" in making most decisions. In the first place, most people are almost totally uninformed about most public issues, and therefore have no real "will" regarding what should be done. They may have generalized ideas about what "the good society" would be like, but these are rarely translated into desires for specific policies on the detailed levels where most decisions must be made. Moreover, even if people were informed enough to have definite opinions, they would most likely not agree with one another. As Duncan Black has shown, any decision involving more than one variable

will almost certainly engender such diverse opinions that no one
alternative will be more pleasing to a majority than every other
one; that is, "circular majorities" will exist.[4]   In such cases it is
unclear which "will" of which people the government official
should follow. Then again, it may happen that a majority of
citizens have definite preferences, and agree on some policy, but
the intensity of their preferences is not so great as that of the
opposing minority. In such instances the majority might be
better off if they let the minority have their way, and then exacted
compensatory payment from that minority. Hence an enlightened
public official may not follow a specific majority preference even
when it exists.[5]   Finally, because public opinion often lags behind
swiftly changing events, the citizenry's preference for a given policy
may be based on ignorance of what is really happening, as has been
argued by Walter Lippmann.[6] Therefore, even if people know
enough to have definite views, and most of them agree on what
should be done, the policy they propose may still be the wrong
one for better informed public officials to carry out. Clearly, these
handicaps usually make it impractical for government officials
to consult the "will of the people." Proponents of the rationalist
view have apparently confused the minimal consensus underlying
democratic government with the detailed public-interest conceptions called for in making day-to-day policy decisions. There is
a "popular will" regarding the minimal consensus, but this consensus is in most cases far too vague to be a guide for detailed
policies.

On the other hand, the rationalists are right that a government

4 Duncan Black and R. A. Newing, *Committee Decisions with Complementary
Valuation* (London 1951).

5 For a discussion of government decision-making strategies see *An Economic
Theory of Democracy* (cited above, note 1) Chapter 4. Further discussions of problems that arise from differing intensities of preference are presented by Gordon
Tullock, "Problems of Majority Voting," in *Journal of Political Economy*, vol. 67
(December 1959) pp. 571–79; by Anthony Downs, "In Defense of Majority Voting,"
ibid., vol. 69 (April 1961) pp. 192–99; and by Gordon Tullock, "Reply to a Tradi-
tionalist," *ibid.*, vol. 69 (April 1961) pp. 200–03.

6 Walter Lippmann, *The Public Philosophy* (Boston 1955).

policy that is "in the public interest" must in the long run be approved of by the majority of citizens because they believe it to be beneficial to themselves. Experience has taught people living in democracies that they cannot allow the officials to be the sole judges of whether their actions are beneficial to the citzenry; democracies were established precisely to avoid this situation. The citizens have empowered themselves to pass such judgment periodically by means of popular elections. In order to stay in office, government officials must periodically persuade a majority of voters to approve of their actions, either by shaping their actions to conform to a majority's preconceived notions of what should be done, or by altering the preconceived notions of enough voters that the policies chosen appear satisfactory. In either case the result must be a degree of conformity between "the popular will" and the decision of government officials, or a new government will replace the existing one.

Idealist theory, like that of the rationalists, provides no concrete guide for choosing specific policies in the public interest, but it does embody a significant insight into the government decision-making process. Idealists believe that government officials should perceive the proper course for government action directly from considering a set of absolute values. The crucial questions are thus what standard of values is the proper one, how a person translates such values into concrete policy decisions, and what kind of relationship exists between the decision-makers and the citizenry.

Apparently, idealists assume there is one set of absolute values that is "proper" for government officials to use, though they do not agree what it is. Some, like Walter Lippmann, attempt to link these values to concepts of natural law. In our pluralistic society, however, this assumption again seems to confuse the minimal consensus with the more detailed content of the public interest. As was pointed out earlier, the minimal consensus does contain a set of personal and political behavior rules that are "absolutely" necessary for the functioning of a democratic political system.   Therefore every citizen who places a high ethical value on the continuance of democracy rightly regards these rules as absolute ethical principles operative in the political sphere.   However, many of these principles are relatively vague and generalized. Furthermore, in a pluralistic society it is not realistic to expect any consensus either on all ultimate values or on detailed policies (and even in a relatively homogeneous society some policy details will always be equivocal).   The minimal consensus, since it includes only certain rules of behavior and generalized policies for social action, is insufficient to provide detailed direction for government decision-making.   It is conceivable that officials will use for this purpose detailed "absolute" principles of their own concerning the welfare of society as a whole, but in such cases they are employing their personal ethical principles rather than any set of principles that the preponderant majority in the society recognizes as "absolutely" valid.

There are nevertheless important germs of truth in idealist theory.   In the first place, when officials must use some type of decision rule not closely tied to public opinion, they must, as pointed out above, keep in mind the necessity of rationalizing the results in terms of at least an ostensible concept of the common good, since such rationalization may some day be required by the pressure of public opinion (in such forms as a congressional investigation, for example).   Moreover, in those decisions that may to some degree involve the survival of democracy, the decision-makers are required by their own self-interest to implement that survival, and they are here acting in the public interest as well, since survival of the system is in the interest of everyone except revolutionaries.   Finally, even though motives are not identical with functions, government officials are aware that their function is widely defined as action in the public interest, as is clearly attested to by innumerable statements from them.   As a consequence, it is certainly likely that an official will in time develop at least a limited set of values with which to rationalize his actions, and in some cases he may actually reverse his normal decision-making priority and derive policy directly from these values. In fact, as he develops a more elaborate set of values with which to rationalize, it may become difficult for him to decide when he is rationalizing and when he is actually basing his decisions on these values.

The above reasoning implies that there is at least a little bit of idealism in every government decision-maker; that is, at least some of his decisions (conceivably most or even all of them, but at least some) are based on a direct application of absolute values in a manner corresponding closely to idealist theory. This conclusion is especially important in regard to the leadership function of government officials. An official, acting as a specialist in the division of labor, is usually in a far better position than the average citizen to know what alternative policies exist and what their consequences might be. In complex and rapidly changing policy situations, his information advantage may often lead him to perceive that a policy presently favored by the majority would in fact be detrimental to their real interests, whereas a policy they do not favor would in fact benefit them in the long run. Only because a government official has developed, however cynically, some concept of the public interest independent of current public opinion will he be able to make such judgments. Having perceived a discrepancy between what the majority now want and what will turn out to be best for them, he can do one of three things, each of which involves certain risks.

One course is to say nothing to change their views, and carry out actions consistent with those views. This involves the risk that the majority will eventually realize a poor policy has been adopted, and will blame him. Second, he can say nothing to change their views, but carry out the actions he believes consistent with their best interests. This course involves the risk that the majority will not realize what their best interests are, and will blame him for acting against their current views. Finally, he can attempt to change their views through information and persuasion, so that they will prefer the actions he believes best for

them, and meanwhile carry out those actions.   This also involves
the risk that the majority will blame him, but the probabilities
are different from those in the second case; the majority are more
likely to recognize he is acting against their current views, but
they are also more likely to change those views because of his
persuasion.

The last of these courses embodies the function of leadership—
a vital function for democracies threatened by hostile social
systems or by internally disruptive forces. The ability to exercise
such leadership demands that officials, no matter what their
motive, have some concept of the public interest similar to that
espoused by idealists.   There is one important distinction, however, between this concept and the idealist view.   Idealists state
that the set of values to be used should be the one and only best set.
In the process I have outlined, the sets of values are those conceived by each government decision-maker to be most effective
in attaining his goals of keeping his conduct within the limits
indicated by the minimal consensus and keeping the system going,
and in following whatever additional decision rule he uses, such
as getting reelected, avoiding public censure, or advancing the
interests of a particular group.   Hence, apart from the fact that
the set of values he adopts must contain those "absolute" values
in the minimal consensus necessary for democracy, there need be
no way of telling whether the set adopted is the one and only best
set.   Only the ultimate survival of the system and popular approval
in the next election (assuming he seeks reelection) can determine
whether the values employed were "correct enough" to have accomplished these goals.

The third school of thought on public interest—the realist
school—also contributes some valuable insights to our understanding of this concept. The so-called Bentleyan realists, who
view the public interest as merely a slogan adopted by different
pressure groups to disguise their own particular interests, are right
in implying that each actor on the public scene is likely to advance
his own version of the public interest, and that there is no a

priori way to designate any one of these views as the one and only
best. Nevertheless, there are times, as we have seen, when the
existence of individual concepts of the public interest is extremely
important in the successful operation of democracy. These individual concepts, derived from individual values, are what is stressed
by the psychological realists, and such values of the decision-maker
are indeed involved in the process of creating government policy,
no matter what primary motive we attribute to him. Finally, the
due-process realists argue, as we have seen, that a policy is in the
public interest if it is arrived at through a process that allows
everyone likely to be affected by it to have a voice in its formation
—thereby making for the most peaceful possible acceptance of the
resulting decisions. Thus they rest their analysis ultimately on
the desirability of maintaining the continuity and stability of the
system—in short, its survival. This point too was expressed above.
Except in rare cases, however, detailed policy choices cannot be
made on this basis. It is not often clear what choices will maximize
the probability of long-run or even short-run survival of democracy;
a given choice is likely to have some survival implications but a
great many other implications as well.

Even after examining all three schools of thought described by
Schubert, we cannot explicitly answer the question "What is the
public interest?" in a way that everyone will agree upon. Nevertheless, the analysis illuminates the nature of the concept, and
may serve as background for the exploration of a further question.

Public Interest versus Private Interests

Even the most fanatic idealist would hardly espouse some policy
as "in the public interest" which did not ever benefit a single
person, including himself. Thus, no matter what method is used
in a given society for deciding which policies are in the public
interest, every one of these policies must redound to someone's
private advantage. For that person (or those persons), the given
policy creates no divergence between private and public interest.

Nevertheless, each person plays a number of different roles in his

THE PUBLIC INTEREST   19

social life, and each role involves a slightly different set of goals from each other role.   Hence even within the mind of a given individual there may be significant "conflicts of interests," because the goals of his different "private" roles are inconsistent.   Even within one role he may experience conflicts between short-run and long-run private interests.   Thus, for each person, merely deciding what his own private interest consists of may be an exceedingly difficult task.   He has to weight the importance of different sets of goals implicit in each of his roles by means of some ultimate standard, which economists have labeled his "utility function." In essence, each person faces within himself the same type of problem faced by society as a whole: the reconciliation of conflict-ing interests among different viewpoints so as to achieve one effective policy for each issue.   If he is a rational person he has, however, one crucial advantage over society as a whole: a single set of ultimate values by which to judge the importance of his various roles.   Even if this standard is not explicit in his mind, he creates an ad hoc version of it by arriving at policy preferences (in so far as he is not completely apathetic about policy).

Thus, in regard to any particular issue, each person can identify the government policy he believes to be most beneficial to his "private interest," by choosing whatever alternative appears to give him the greatest net gain in utility in light of all his private roles in society.   In contrast, his "pure" view of which policies are in the public interest is in theory based on the values appro-priate to only one of his roles—that of citizen.   In this role, under my definition, he views society as a unit so that he can consider its functioning in relation to its overall goals *as he perceives them.* He does not weight any one part of the society (such as himself) any more than any other part, for such weighting, however appro-priate to his other roles, is by definition inappropriate to a citizen qua citizen.   His personal values influence what he believes to be the proper goals of society seen as a unit, and, as we shall see presently, even the role of "pure" citizenship is not entirely di-vorced from self-interest, but the fact remains that as citizen he regards society as a whole instead of himself as the appropriate focus of concern.

This analysis of how each person determines his own private interest and his "pure" view of the public interest is of course a theoretical abstraction, not a literal description of the thought processes of real persons. Nevertheless, if the ideas of private and public interests have meaning, they must be capable of formulation by individuals, and this process will necessarily resemble the one described—at least in structure, if not consciously. We may say, therefore, that it is possible for a man's private interests to diverge from his "pure" view of the public interest even if he has perfect information about real-world conditions. The divergency is increased, however, by the cost of information, both in time and in money. Because acquiring information is costly, men are never fully informed about any issue: there is always more to know that might influence each decision. The resulting ignorance creates a potential gap between what a man perceives as private and public interests and what he would perceive them to be if he had perfect information. On the general principle that greater information normally enables anyone to make better decisions, this gap has certain characteristics and consequences that have an important bearing on political behavior, as I have tried to show elsewhere.[7]

One such consequence of ignorance is that it makes long-run considerations more difficult to perceive than short-run considerations. The world is so complex that far distant ramifications of any present action are usually much more difficult to predict than its immediate effects—which are themselves often hard to foresee. This inherent uncertainty about the future, which can be reduced but never eliminated by more information about the present world, causes people to weight immediate consequences, as opposed to ultimate ones, more heavily than they would if they had perfect knowledge. A second consequence of ignorance is

[7] Anthony Downs, "Why the Government Budget is Too Small in a Democracy," in *World Politics,* vol. 12 (July 1960) pp. 541–63.

that men concentrate on getting information likely to have a high pay-off. Such data are those relevant to decisions that are of direct importance to the persons concerned, and that their views have some probability of influencing. The classic example is the tariff. Producers are always well informed about tariffs in their industry, whereas consumers, less vitally involved, are usually poorly informed about them. Furthermore, producers realize that very few persons are informed about their product, and hence feel they have a good chance of influencing decisions concerning it; this increases their probable pay-off from being informed.

The expected pay-off from knowing about the private interests associated with certain personal roles—particularly the income-earning role—is much larger than the expected pay-off from knowing what the public interest should consist of. In each man's role as citizen he is confronted by two facts that discourage the investment of many resources in obtaining information: first, there are so many issues that he cannot possibly be well informed on even a small fraction of them; and second, there are so many other citizens that the probability of his influence being significant in the final outcome is small. Therefore almost every citizen is much better informed about factors that impinge on his private life, especially on the way he earns his income, than he is about public affairs in general. This outcome stems not from any irrationality, stupidity, or lack of patriotism, but from an economically rational approach to the cost of information.

If most people are poorly informed in their roles as citizens but relatively well informed in their roles as income-earners, they are likely to make two different kinds of errors in judging what the public interest consists of. The first is selecting the wrong policies to achieve their ultimate goals; this leads to random variations from the "correct" policy, that is, the policy any given person would choose were he perfectly informed about the situation. The second kind of error introduces a non-random bias, because it results from each person's formulating his view of the public interest in terms of those things he knows best. This bias is commonly recognized concerning each man's view of his private interests. But the distortion will occur even in his role as a citizen, that is, even when he is trying to make policy judgments not influenced by his own particular economic or social interests, for his particular interests limit the kind of information he has with which to judge. That men cannot entirely escape from the bias imparted to their perception of reality by their particular locus in society is a well recognized doctrine in the sociology of knowledge.[8]

So far, we have discussed "conflict of interests" in terms of three divergences: that between each man's view of his private interests and what this view would be if he were perfectly informed (leading him to give excessive weight to short-run factors relative to long-run ones); that between his "pure" view of the public interest and what this view would be if he were perfectly informed (leading him not only to excessive concern with short-run factors but also to errors arising from ignorance and to undue stress on how policy affects those social sectors in which he is personally engaged); and that between his information concerning his private interest and his information concerning the public interest (leading him to misjudgments in his "pure" view of the public interest, both through lack of knowledge and through the bias imparted by his locus in the social division of labor).

Actually, none of these divergences is normally referred to by the term "conflict of interest" as applied to public officials. The common usage of this term denotes the possibility of exploiting the powers of office to further the official's private interest as opposed to the public interest as viewed by others (which may or may not coincide with the public interest as he himself views it). This type of conflict is obviously disconcerting to theorists who posit that officials are normally motivated solely by their zeal to carry out the public interest. However, in my model of government, officials are assumed to be normally motivated primarily

[8] The best known exposition of this view is in Karl Mannheim, *Ideology and Utopia* (New York 1936).

by their own private interests, defined as gaining and enjoying the power, income, and prestige of office; therefore they are expected to act so as to further those interests. If their actions diverge too far from the concept of the public interest held by others (especially by voters), this divergence may affect their ability to stay in office, as was stressed above. Therefore the type of conflict usually denoted by the term "conflict of interests" has no special significance to our analysis.

But there is another type of interest conflict that is very important to this discussion: the divergence between one man's view of the public interest and other men's views of it. If each person's conception is biased by his particular locus in the division of labor, even when abstracted from his self-interest, then the more complex the division of labor becomes, the more will people's views of the public interest differ. Thus economic progress, by increasing the number of specialized points of view in society, diminishes the degree of unanimity about social policy that can be expected to prevail. If we assumed that each person espoused as his view of the public interest what was in fact his net private-interest position, this tendency toward differentiation among views of the "proper" social policies would become even more prominent. Everyone would then base his views of proper public policy not on considerations of the welfare of society as a whole as he saw it, but on considerations of his own private welfare alone. Whichever approach we uphold, it is clear that the tendency toward social differentiation caused by the division of labor lies at the root of the widespread disagreement about the public interest encountered in all modern democracies.

To be sure, economic progress also creates forces that mitigate its divisive effects. First, by producing increasingly standardized products and social surroundings it reduces the regional diversity so often found in "young" democracies. Second, specialization makes each person so dependent on the efforts of others that he cannot long withdraw his cooperation except under extreme stress; therefore he is relatively amenable to accepting government actions carried out in the name of the public interest, even if they are detrimental to his own private interests. Third, the greater the complexity of a society the more difficult it is for the citizens to keep well informed, and this very difficulty has a functional advantage in relation to the stability of the system. Most citizens are not able to concentrate their attention on protesting every government policy that harms their private interests to some degree, and the resultant ignorance prevents the sharpening of conflicts on relatively trivial invasions of private advantage.

Nevertheless, standardization, interdependency, and inescapable ignorance do not overcome all the problems created by the social divergency inherent in an intensive division of labor. To offset this divergency, a successful democratic society (one capable of passing the test of survival) must continuously indoctrinate its citizens with the values contained in its basic minimal consensus. They must be taught sufficiently similar intermediate values that their behavior, by and large, is consistent with the system. Such behavior must include willingness to make personal sacrifices to keep the system from perishing, adherence to a few basic moral rules, observation of the political constitution, and agreement on a vague set of policy principles. These values must be given enough moral force in the mind of each person that he usually overcomes the temptation always faced by every member of an organization: the desire to break the rules in order to procure some short-run personal advantage at the expense of furthering the long-run purposes of the organization, which are themselves ultimately beneficial to him. Men naturally tend to weight short-run considerations more heavily than long-run ones, and their own preferences more heavily than the preferences of others. These tendencies must be so resisted by moral suasion, backed by the threat of reprisal, that the basic rules predominate in the operation of the system, thus making behavior tolerably predictable.

Any description of a democratic system which does not include some mechanism for such self-perpetuation is an incomplete description. It does not explain why people within it keep obeying the rules that make it possible. This omission is, in my opinion, the biggest single failing of my own economic theory of democracy. However, it is not possible in this paper to describe all the social devices that would have to be built into the model to provide it with the means of perpetuating itself. Such description would require extensive theorizing in sociology, psychology, anthropology, and communications theory. Furthermore, given the present state of empirical knowledge about what social elements are necessary for democracy, it is by no means certain that this theorizing would lead to the creation of a viable structure. Therefore at present this deficiency in the economic model of democracy can be remedied only by simply assuming that some such indoctrination and enforcement mechanisms exist in each democratic society, and that they function successfully.

Implications for the Economic Model of Politics

The foregoing analysis suggests that the public interest, at least as a concept, plays an important role in democratic politics. Yet my analysis in *An Economic Theory of Democracy* rarely mentions the term "public interest," and certainly does not appear to assign it any key role in politics, either as a motive or as an instrument. Does this mean that the model in the book is fundamentally wrong, as its critics suggest? In answering this question I contend that the role of public interest as a concept is in fact dealt with at great length in the book, but under the name "ideology." Nevertheless, the book does not fully explore the role of the public-interest concept in government decision-making, as has been attempted in this article; hence the theories originally advanced in the model need certain clarifications. I believe that after these changes are made, the basic structure of the original model remains valid, both as a causal model useful for predicting certain types of behavior and as a heuristic tool providing insights into the relationships of the various parts of society.

In this article I have argued that government decision-makers form views of the public interest, at least for purposes of rationalizing actions actually decided on for other reasons. They do this because voters expect them to be able to rationalize their actions in this manner, and they must meet voters' expectations to stay in office. In *An Economic Theory of Democracy* it was argued that political parties form ideologies because some voters want them to do so. By studying ideologies instead of individual issues, these voters can save resources that would otherwise have to be invested in more detailed information. Thus in both cases, each government decision-maker formulates a concept of what ought to be done, not because he wants to carry out the policies embodied in the concept as ends in themselves, but because he finds it expedient to please voters by formulating this concept. (In my original analysis, the decision-making unit was the party rather than the individual official, since I assumed all individuals within the party had identical preference functions.)

True, there are some differences between my original concept of ideologies and the concept of the public interest described in this article. In particular, ideologies were conceived as relatively broad and general, whereas the public interest is conceived as very detailed. But no change in the motivation of government decision-makers is required to alter the original analysis of ideologies and apply it to the public interest as well. Thus the decision-making process described in the original model, in so far as it concerns government decision-makers, fits the analysis in this article very well.

But there are two other aspects of political action regarding which the original model does not so clearly fit the ideas developed in the present analysis. First, I have argued here that each individual citizen develops a "pure" view of the public interest based on seeing society as a unit and not weighting himself more than others; this was called his view in his role as citizen. It was also pointed out that he has a net private-interest position developed from all of his non-citizen roles, in which he normally does weight his own preferences more than those of others. But which of these views dominates his political decision-making, that is, his voting and lobbying?

Before answering this question it is necessary to consider the motivation underlying each person's role as citizen. Why should he develop a view of society's goals as though society were a unit, with no extra weight attached to his own preferences? The traditional answer is that such a "pure" view is necessary for good citizenship, and good citizenship is the duty of every person, because without it society would not work well, and everyone would suffer in the long run. Thus it might be argued that the ultimate motive for good citizenship, even for the most pious patriots, is the long-run self-interest of the individual. Carrying out his role as citizen is one of the many ways in which each person manifests his long-run self-interest; hence this role appears to have the same basic motive as the roles in which he considers his private interests alone. But if every person voted only on the basis of his citizenship role, self-interest in the traditional sense (the sense used to explain maximization of profits, for example) would not be operative in the political sphere. Instead, all disagreements over what policies are optimal would be explained solely by the fact that different citizens have different ultimate values, different positions in the division of labor, and different current information—not by any desire whatever on their part to further their own interests at the expense of others. This conclusion in my opinion so manifestly contradicts all political experience that I reject it outright.

A more plausible possibility is that the view of the public interest on which each citizen actually bases his political decisions is his "total net" position. That is, it represents the balance of all his roles, both private and public. In formulating this total net position he considers the "pure" view of the public interest derived from his citizenship role simply as one of the many views of proper government action he has developed from all of his roles. Since nearly all of his other roles are primarily private ones (that is, they represent his self-interest), the ultimate view of the public interest on which he bases his political actions represents the "pure" view he has developed as a citizen modified by the views he has developed to meet his private needs.

At first glance this conclusion leaves us in the dark about whether to predict each person's behavior from what appears to be his private interest or from what appears to be his "pure" view of the public interest. Apparently we cannot make any predictions about his political behavior at all, except in those cases when his private interests and his views of the public interest coincide. Much of this ambiguity can be removed, however, by specifying certain circumstances in which his "pure" view of the public interest is likely to determine his behavior, and others in which his private interests will probably rule. Each citizen's "pure" view of the public interest will probably influence him most strongly regarding the following types of government decisions: those on which survival of the system clearly hinges; those that only remotely or indirectly affect his own private interests; and those in which certain policy choices clearly involve abrogation of the rules specified in the minimal consensus (for example, whether to vote for an official who has accepted bribes to overlook faulty construction of schools). Conversely, private interests will probably determine each citizen's political action regarding those policies that have a direct effect on his income, his working conditions, or some other activity with which he is intimately associated (for example, schools and maintenance of property values).

Between these extremes it appears difficult to say, a priori, which considerations are most likely to influence his political action, since there are many policies that involve a mixture of effects on survival, personal income, and the rules of the basic consensus. Nevertheless, the analysis can be extended further. As pointed out earlier, citizens are best informed about those policies that directly affect their incomes, and worst informed about those with no direct effects on them, that is, those most likely to be remote from their own private interests. Thus each citizen will usually be most keenly interested in those policies regarding which his private interests will influence his behavior most strongly, and least interested in those regarding which he is likely to act in accordance with his view of the public interest. In judging the overall performance of the government or the promised performance of its opposition, he will place much heavier weight on policies about which his views are dictated by self-interest. Therefore, in the absence of any specific knowledge about each citizen's particular weights, it is more accurate to predict his political behavior by assuming he will act in accordance with his private interest than to predict it on consideration of his views about the public interest, except in cases clearly involving the survival of the system or its basic values.

This is, in fact, exactly the procedure used in *An Economic Theory of Democracy*. The only modification indicated by the present analysis consists of specifying two types of policy decisions about which we do have a priori indications that the citizen, in judging them, is likely to weight his view of the public interest quite heavily: those involving either survival of the system or clear abrogations of the rules in the minimal consensus. In all other matters we will attain the best results by assuming that voters act in accordance with their self-interest. Again I point out that self-interest is not narrowly defined; it can include highly altruistic behavior that an individual believes he ought to undertake, even at his own expense. For most citizens, however, self-interest does imply that each person will weight his own welfare more than that of others in making decisions.

A similar modification of the model is required regarding decision-making by government officials and politicians. As citizens of the political system, they too have a stake in the continuance of the system—usually an extraordinarily high stake, since they support themselves by operating it. Therefore, in making government policy decisions, their "pure" view of the public interest will tend to prevail over their private interests in regard to the same classes of decision that affect other citizens in this way:

decisions on which survival of the system clearly hinges; those that only remotely affect their personal interests, because considerations of votes give no clear imperative for any one policy choice; and those in which certain policy choices clearly involve abrogation of the rules in the minimal consensus (for example, murdering opposition candidates). Thus modified, the model can explain such policy choices as President Truman's ordering United States troops to defend Korea, even though he undoubtedly realized that this act would cause heavy losses of political support for his party and himself. Since he believed the survival of the system to be at stake, he based his decision on his view of the public interest rather than on the narrower motives that *An Economic Theory of Democracy* ascribes to all government decisions. There are of course many decisions in which these modifying considerations are only partially involved, and it is difficult then to predict the weights the official will apply. And there are many in which purely political considerations are so remote or so evenly balanced that the decision can be made on the basis of what is then a residual factor: the official's view of the public interest. But in the absence of a priori knowledge to the contrary, one can safely predict that the official will make decisions on the basis of vote considerations except when the survival of the system or a gross violation of its basic rules is clearly involved.

It might be objected that these modifications of the model introduce an element of altruism into the political sphere, for if officials or citizens-as-voters give any weight whatever to their "pure" views of the public interest, they are not motivated by the same unadulterated self-interest that spurs profit-maximizing entrepreneurs and utility-maximizing consumers in economic theory —and in my original model. In other words, by postulating motivations and behavior in the public sector inconsistent with those operative in private sectors, the model exhibits the very fault it was designed to cure. The easy answer is to state that politicians and voters who act to save the system or preserve its basic rules are really also motivated by self-interest. For example, it is more to the interest of a politician to live under a democratic system in which his party is out of office than to keep his party in office for a while but then be forced to live under a non-democratic system; hence those who see an inconsistency about his acting here in accordance with his "pure" view of the public interest are merely confusing long-run with short-run motivation.

This answer does not, however, penetrate to the heart of the matter, for there is indeed a difference between private and public decisions.   Every system of social behavior is based on a set of rules governing the conduct of its participants.   If enough participants violate enough of the rules enough of the time, the system ceases to work.   Yet every participant sooner or later encounters a situation in which he can make a short-run gain by violating some rule, and the only loss he sees is the contribution of this violation to the general breakdown of the system—which in most cases appears extremely small.   A preponderant majority of the system's participants must be willing to resist such temptations most of the time if the system is to work.   And their resistance must ultimately be supported by an ethical commitment on their part.   The necessity of this commitment explains why all societies indoctrinate their members with such non-rational props as internal guilt and reward feelings to buttress the dominant rules.   Such rules operate, of course, in private as well as public affairs, yet their ultimate protection lies in the sphere of the state, because the state controls the use of force.   This is also the sphere of the public interest. Therefore any realistic consideration of politics must take into account the necessity for this non-rational commitment, and indicate that it in fact affects behavior at least some of the time.

Although this commitment can be interpreted as a form of self-interest, it is a form different from that assumed to operate in the private sectors of decision-making in traditional economic theory. It is supposed that private consumers and producers obey the law for reasons of self-gain and because it is enforced by the state, not because of any moral commitment on their part.   Thus it is true that a new element has been introduced into the model by recognizing the existence of this commitment in public actions. But this does not mean that the model is thereby made either internally inconsistent or realistically inoperative. The amendment merely brings into the open the fact that every social system implicitly contains such a moral commitment, even if it is not overtly recognized—whereas this commitment remained concealed in the autonomous and unexplained government sector of traditional economic theory. Furthermore, I am not returning to the fallacy that *all* actions of government officials and voters are dictated by the desire to maximize social welfare, the public good, or some other synonym for the public interest. In fact, the central hypothesis remains that government officials set policy in order to win or retain office; the amended model merely recognizes an exception in those few instances where their moral commitment to democracy as a social system overrides their short-run self-interest. The distinction between motive and function, which differentiates the economic theory of democracy from previous economic theories of government decision-making, is retained.

A further point must be stressed. Just as recognition of a moral commitment in the political sphere does not necessarily introduce an inconsistent element of altruism, recognition of the weight of self-interest should not be construed as a cynical mandate to public officials to eschew any thoughts of the public interest in making government decisions. On the contrary, as a citizen I believe officials ought to use their views of the public interest as a major guidepost in making decisions, within the limits wisely imposed by the electoral system. I do not agree with Schubert that we should quit talking or thinking about the public interest merely because we cannot agree on what it is. My political model, however, is designed not to describe how men ought to behave, but how they actually will behave. Since I believe that men are inherently selfish to some extent, I have designed the model to take account of this fact. As social scientists we should analyze the world realistically so that, as ethical men, we can design social mechanisms that utilize men's actual motives to produce social

conditions as close as possible to our ideal of "the good society."
Failure to be realistic about human nature would lead us to design
social mechanisms that do not achieve their desired ends. Conversely, abandoning ideals leads to cynical nihilism. I hope my
amended model will provide greater insight into how to go about
making the real world more like the ideal one.

Significance for Current World Politics

The purpose of this article has been to place the concept of the
public interest in its proper setting in regard to both real-world
democracies and theoretical models depicting them. It is my contention that the economic theory of democracy, as amended above,
is a useful tool for perceiving just what role this concept can be
expected to play in a democratic political system. However, the
theory has been strongly criticized by Gerhard Colm (note 1, above)
for failing to recognize the importance of leadership and citizen
participation in a democracy. Colm argues that leaders take the
initiative in developing programs they believe to be in the public
interest, and then try to convince voters of this fact, just as entrepreneurs invent new products and then try to create a demand
for them. In so far as such invention of policy involves survival
of the system, it is consistent with the amended theory I have
stated. The theory can even explain further innovations by politicians, if they are motivated by the desire to differentiate their
political product from that of their opponents, thereby winning
votes. Nevertheless, there is a significant difference between
Colm's view of leaders who act in the public interest regardless
of public opinion, and then persuade the public to approve their
acts, and my view of leaders who are afraid to venture too far from
the public's present views because they might lose votes.

Judging by the lack of imagination recently shown by democratic societies in combating totalitarianism and solving their own
internal problems, I believe that my view is more realistic. One
of democracy's basic problems today is freeing government decision-makers from the necessity of conforming their policies to

the erroneous views of a public whose members have chosen to remain uninformed politically, because becoming informed is not economically rational.[9] We need to give our government officials enough independent power to tackle our basic problems with originality and initiative, without at the same time giving them enough power to develop a dictatorship. Colm is certainly right that we have a dire need for original and creative leadership. But, as I have stressed, the economic theory of democracy is designed to analyze the actual working of the system, not its desired working. Therefore this theory emphasizes the critical problems we face in developing the kind of leadership we need, instead of assuming we have already solved those problems and obtained that leadership.

As for citizen participation, the model admittedly paints a discouraging picture. It indicates that the rational course of action for most individual citizens is to remain ignorant about public affairs. And if public opinion is ignorant, and government officials are tied to public opinion in the creation of policy, the possibilities for successful solutions of our problems appear less than optimal. In traditional democratic theory, citizens participated in government by becoming well informed about current issues and expressing their views to their representatives, who then created policies that mirrored these views. Because the citizenry was well informed, the resulting policies were expected to be effective in meeting basic social needs. The model I have presented does not deny that better government (that is, closer conformity of government policy to the majority's real needs) would actually occur if everyone were well informed; in fact, it affirms this. But it also contends that the individual's moral commitment to the preservation of the system, though effective in getting large numbers of people to vote, is not likely to extend to the point where he spends a great deal of his resources becoming and remaining politically informed. Surveys of the amount of

[9] The question whether being politically well informed is economically rational (that is, efficient) for individual citizens is discussed at length in *An Economic Theory of Democracy*, Chapter 13.

current information known to large numbers of citizens certainly support this argument.

Thus the economic theory of democracy points up the critical difficulties inherent in a modern democracy regarding leadership and citizen participation. It does not pose any easy solutions to these difficulties. In fact, its conclusions are quite alarming when they are contrasted with the nature of leadership and participation under totalitarian systems. The leaders of a totalitarian system possess many of the possibilities of initiative, flexibility, and capability of producing social sacrifice which our leaders lack. This is true for a simple reason: in a totalitarian system those who make the decisions calling for sacrifice do not have to make the sacrifices themselves or obtain the consent of those who do make them. In a democracy the ultimate policymakers—the voters—are also the ultimate sacrifice-sufferers, and thus it is natural for democracies to be more reluctant to adopt social policies calling for rapid change or individual sacrifice than totalitarian states. According to the amended economic theory of democracy, the average citizen is likely to make such sacrifices only when he feels the survival of the system is threatened. Since normally he is poorly informed, by the time he realizes that the system is being threatened, it may be too late.

Similarly, totalitarian states can utilize different and much easier methods of fostering individual participation. By such means as unitary control over mass media, giant rallies and meetings, national campaigns for public policy goals put over with the same enthusiasm and skill with which toothpaste and brassieres are sold in the United States, and constant reiteration of the individual's stake in social performance, a totalitarian government can produce in its citizens strong feelings of belonging and participation. Furthermore, attainment of these feelings does not require the citizens to become acquainted with the real complexities of political life, or to make any decisions regarding those difficult issues that governments everywhere must face. Although this form of participation seems a mere sham to those who want the citizenry

to make final policy decisions, it can at least counteract the tendency toward apathy and social inaction inherent in the problem of
rational ignorance. Here again, a totalitarian state has a tremendously greater capability of mobilizing its people into the kind of
social action efficacious in solving many basic problems, particularly those engendered by rapid industrialization.

Of course, democracies have no monopoly on problems. Undoubtedly an analogous "economic theory of communism" would
expose equally basic difficulties inherent in the operation of our
rival system. Even if it did not, we would still prefer democracy,
since the problems of democracy are the inevitable costs of secur-
ing its greatest benefit: a government responsive to the needs and
desires of those it governs. But the high value we place on this
goal should not blind us to the fact that it imposes on us certain
handicaps in our current worldwide competition with totalitarianism. These handicaps are clearly illuminated by the economic
theory of democracy. Because the first step toward insuring the
survival of our system is understanding its real advantages and
limitations, I believe this theory is a useful tool, however pessimistic its conclusions may seem.

[5]

THE JOURNAL OF
POLITICAL ECONOMY

Volume LXXIII	JUNE 1965	Number 3

A THEORY OF LARGE MANAGERIAL FIRMS

R. JOSEPH MONSEN, JR., AND ANTHONY DOWNS[1]

College of Business Administration, University of Washington, and
Real Estate Research Corporation, Los Angeles, California

I. INTRODUCTION

FOR a long time, there has been dissatisfaction with the traditional theory of the firm and its basic axiom that firms maximize profits.[2] This article attempts to propound a more realistic alternative applicable to large corporate firms.

In our opinion, the traditional theory of the firm really deals with only *one type* of firm: the small, owner-managed firm. But since the inception of this theory, several other types of firms have come into being that differ from the traditional type in both owner-management relationships and size. Moreover, these other types of firms are now economically more significant than the traditional type in terms of the magnitude of the resources which they control.

Distinguishing between types of firms is important because the behavior of each firm with respect to profits depends upon certain elements of its internal

[1] All views expressed in this paper are those of the authors and do not necessarily reflect the views of either the University of Washington or the Real Estate Research Corporation. The authors are developing, separately, in forthcoming studies a number of the ideas outlined in this article.

[2] See R. L. Hall and C. J. Hitch, "Price Theory and Business Behaviour," *Oxford Economic Papers*, May, 1939; B. Higgins, "Elements of Indeterminacy in the Theory of Non-Profit Competition," *American Economic Review*, September, 1939; T. Parsons, "The Motivations of Economic Activity," *Canadian Journal of Economics and Political Science*, May, 1940; K. W. Rothschild, "Price Theory and Oligopoly," *Economic Journal*, September, 1947; M. W. Reder, "A Reconsideration of the Marginal Productivity Theory," *Journal of Political Economy*, October, 1947; W. Fellner, *Competition among the Few* (New York: Alfred A. Knopf, 1949); George Katona, *Psychological Analysis of Economic Behaviors* (New York: McGraw-Hill Book Co., 1951); K. E. Boulding, "Implications for General Economics of More Realistic Theories of the Firm," *American Economic Review, Supplement*, May, 1952; T. Scitovsky, "A Note on Profit Maximization and Its Implications," reprinted in *Readings in Price Theory* (Homewood, Ill.: Richard D. Irwin, Inc., 1952); A. A. Papandreau, "Some Basic Problems in the Theory of the Firm," in B. F. Haley (ed.), *A Survey of Contemporary Economics*, Vol. II (Homewood, Ill.: Richard D. Irwin, Inc., 1952); C. A. Hickman and M. H. Kuhn, *Individuals, Groups and Economic Behavior* (New York: Dryden Press, 1956); H. A. Simon, *Administrative Behavior* (New York: Macmillan Co., 1957); W. Baumol, *Business Behavior, Value and Growth*, (New York: Macmillan Co., 1959); and Robin Marris, "A Model of the 'Managerial' Enterprise," *Quarterly Journal of Economics*, May, 1963.

221

structure. In firms whose managers are not also their owners there may be a divergence of interest between the managers and the owners in certain situations. Such a divergence can cause firms to deviate from profit-maximizing behavior. Size also influences each firm's behavior regarding profit maximization. Very large firms must develop bureaucratic management structures to cope with their administrative problems. But such structures inevitably introduce certain conflicts of interest between men in different positions within them. These conflicts arise because the goals of middle and lower management are different from those of top management. The introduction of these additional goals into the firm's decision-making process also leads to systematic deviations from profit-maximizing behavior.

In this article, we will explore the specific ways in which firm size and goal divergence between owners and managers and among various levels of management cause large-size, corporate firms to deviate from the profit-maximizing behavior posited by the traditional theory of the firm.

II. TYPES OF FIRMS

In most economic theory, questions regarding the relationships among different parts of the firm simply do not arise. Instead, economists generally assume that the firm can be treated as a single person, with a unified and integrated set of motives and the ability to carry out its goals without any wasted effort except that imposed by the technical limitations of production and distribution. There are some exceptions to this viewpoint, but those holding other views have not succeeded in shaking the dominance of the traditional concept.[3] For example, A. A. Berle, Jr., and

Gardiner Means long ago pointed out that the separation of ownership from management created situations which traditional theory was not adequate to deal with.[4] In sociology, a sizable literature has grown up concerning bureaucracy in large organizations, and much of it is applicable to large-scale firms.[5] However, thus far, the theory of bureaucracy and the theory of the firm have not been successfully integrated.

There are so many different kinds of firms in the real world that any method of classifying them is bound to be arbitrary. Nevertheless, we have developed several categories of firms based on two variables: size, and the relationship between the owners of the firm and those who manage it. We have concentrated solely upon these two because they have a direct relationship to the question of whether or not the firm maximizes profits.

Our purpose in using size as a criterion for distinguishing among firms is to separate those with bureaucratic management structures from those that do not have such structures. Therefore, we will consider any firm *small* if it has less

[3] One of the most important recent treatments of the subject dealt with in this paper is that of Oliver E. Williamson, whose analysis in certain respects is similar to our own. While the authors have benefited from his perceptive criticism of later drafts, the present paper was originally written completely independently of Williamson's work. His whole theory is presented in *The Economics of Discretionary Behavior: Managerial Objectives in a Theory of the Firm* (Englewood Cliffs, N.J.: Prentice-Hall, Inc., 1964), and a summary appears in "Managerial Discretion and Business Behavior," *American Economic Review*, December, 1963.

[4] *The Modern Corporation and Private Property* (New York: Macmillan Co., 1932). A later work on the same subject is Berle's *Power without Property* (New York: Harcourt, Brace & Co., 1959).

[5] An extensive bibliography is presented in Peter M. Blau and W. Richard Scott, *Formal Organizations* (San Francisco: Chandler Publishing Co., 1962), pp. 258–301.

than 1,000 employees, and *large* if it has 1,000 or more employees. This boundary line between small and large firms is admittedly arbitrary, but it will serve our purposes in the present analysis.

There are also many different relationships between the owners of firms and those who actually manage them (that is, the highest-ranking men in the management structure). As a start toward categorizing these relationships, we propose the following catalogue of firms:

1. *Owner-managed firms* are those managed by the people who own controlling interests in the firm (whether it is a corporation, a partnership, or some other type of organization).
2. *Managerial firms* are those managed by men who do not own anywhere near a controlling interest in them (or any interest at all). Such firms can be further divided into:
   a) *Diffused ownership managerial firms* in which no one person or organized coalition of persons owns a controlling interest in the firm.
   b) *Concentrated ownership managerial firms* in which one person or an organized coalition of persons owns a controlling interest in the firm and (presumably) exercises control over the management. For all purposes of our analysis, such firms are nearly identical with owner-managed firms. Therefore, we will use the term *managerial firms* to refer only to diffused ownership managerial firms.
3. *Non-ownership firms* are those legally considered non-profit organizations. "Ownership" of such firms does not include the legal right to receive earnings from them. Moreover, such firms are usually entirely controlled by trustees or directors with no ownership relation to them at all.
4. *Fiduciarily owned firms* are those whose "owners" are persons making capital payments into the firms primarily for purposes other than receiving income or capital gains therefrom. Examples of such firms are mutual insurance companies and pension funds. The managers of such firms are normally similar to trustees and usually have no significant ownership in the firms themselves.

It seems clear from the above catalogue that the traditional theory of the firm does not apply equally well to all types of firms. For example, it is not obvious that non-ownership firms maximize profits, since they are by definition non-profit organizations. Moreover, fiduciarily owned firms probably have a much stronger orientation toward tempering profit maximization with considerations of security than owner-managed firms. However, our analysis will not deal with these types of firms any further, but will instead concentrate on managerial firms. Our only point in introducing this catalogue of firms— which could undoubtedly be improved and, we hope, will be—is to illustrate our beliefs that (1) different principles of behavior should be formulated for different types of firms, and (2) the traditional principle of profit-maximization really applies to only a limited number of types—even though they may be extremely important.

III. THE BASIC THEORY

A. BACKGROUND STRUCTURE

This article advances a theory about the way that certain firms make decisions under relatively realistic conditions. Specifically, the following conditions will be assumed:

1. The firms involved are large corporations with ownership divided among a great many stockholders. No one stockholder has anywhere near a controlling interest.
2. Each firm has a board of directors elected by its stockholders. This board has ultimate power over the firm's policies and can replace any of its executives (though in some cases it is effectively controlled by those executives).
3. Each firm is operated by a set of managers arranged in a hierarchical pyramid. This pyramid contains at least the following three layers:
   a) *Top management* consists of those few key

executives who are involved in making the basic policy and planning decisions.

b) *Middle management* consists of those operating executives under top management who are responsible for carrying out various specialized tasks within the firm. There may be several horizontal layers within the middle management structure. The lowest level of middle management has direct authority over lower management.

c) *Lower management* consists of supervisory personnel at the foreman or comparable level. Lower management has direct authority over production or lowest-level clerical personnel.

4. Managers (especially top managers) may own stock in their respective firms. However, the proportion of stock which any one manager or group of managers in a firm controls is so small that it does not constitute anywhere near a controlling interest in the firm. Moreover, the stock dividends of each manager comprise a relatively small part of his income in relation to his salary and bonuses.

5. Each firm operates in a world of uncertainty and risk in which knowledge is costly and perfect knowledge normally unobtainable. These conditions prevail regarding both the firm's relations with the rest of the world, and relations among various parts of the firm itself.

6. The degree of oligopoly or monopoly prevalent in each firm's industry is not specified. Our theory does not offer any solution to the oligopoly problem. However, we will assume that (a) each firm operates in a market which contains enough competition so that the firm can conceivably face some risks regarding its long-term survival, but (b) it enjoys enough of a monopolistic position so that it can usually earn profits larger than the "normal" level associated with a perfectly competitive industry.

Under these conditions, there are three classes of decision-makers who can potentially affect a firm's policies and behavior: owners, members of the board of directors, and managers. Since managers are usually represented on the board of directors by the very top executives of the firm, there are really only two auton-omous groups in the firm's decision-making structure: owners and managers. Where ownership is extremely fragmented and no large stockholders exist, the managers often effectively control the board of directors through proxy agreements. However, we assume that the board is sufficiently independent of the managers to punish extremely poor management performance and reward very good performance.

B. CENTRAL HYPOTHESES

The central hypotheses of our theory concern the *motivations* of owners and managers. We believe that traditional theory is correct in assuming that the people who operate business firms are primarily motivated by their own self-interest. But pursuit of self-interest is a characteristic of human persons, not organizations. A *firm* is not a real person, even when incorporated; hence it really cannot have motives or maximize anything. When traditional theorists stated that *firms* maximize profits, they really meant that the *people who run firms* make decisions so as to maximize the profits of the firms. As long as firms were operated by their owners, this assumption was consistent with the self-interest axiom, because the profits of the firms were the main incomes of their owners.

But in most of the largest and most significant modern firms, ownership and management are functions carried out by two entirely separate groups of people. Even management itself is really a combination of functions carried out by different groups. Thus the entity normally referred to as *the firm* has in fact become a number of different subentities. The people in each of these subgroups within the firm are still primarily motivated by self-interest. However, their changed relationship to the firm as a whole has changed the way in which their self-interest leads them to behave regarding the firm's profits. Therefore, our theory is really nothing more than the application of the self-interest axiom in traditional theory to a new type of firm: one in which ownership is separate from management; and management itself consists of a bureaucratic hierarchy containing several layers.

Our two central hypotheses can be stated as follows:

1. *Owners desire to have each firm managed so that it provides a steady income from dividends and gradual appreciation of the market price of the stock.*
2. *Managers act so as to maximize their own lifetime incomes.*

Since these two hypotheses are the foundations of our whole analysis, we will examine each in detail.

C. THE MOTIVATION OF OWNERS

Although every stockholder certainly prefers a rapid rate of advance in the price of his stock to a slow rate, most owners also prefer a slow but steady rise to an erratic combination of rapid rises and equally rapid declines. This is probably true even if the total rise would be slightly higher in the case of erratic movement. A slow but steady rise preserves each owner's ability to get back his original investment plus a profit at any time, whereas up-and-down price movements create uncertainty in his mind about the future price of the stock, thereby creating an apparent risk that he might suffer a loss if he had to sell at a certain moment. Since stockholders typically know far less about the firm's situation than managers, such uncertainty can exist in the minds of stockholders even if the managers know the erratic short-run movements of the stock's price result

from factors which will work out favorably in the long run.

Another important characteristic of owners is their ignorance of the alternative policies available to the firm. Since owners are remote from the firm's actual decision-making, they learn about the firm's performance only ex post, and then only through "official" reports from top management (unless the firm has so blundered that its mistakes have been publicly reported). As a result, owners have no reliable way of determining whether the firm is maximizing its profits and the growth of its stock prices or not. Their only yardstick consists of comparisons with other similar firms. Even this yardstick is an imprecise one, for no two firms are ever exactly alike, and the performance of every firm in any one year is usually conditioned by some unique events applicable to it alone. Therefore, owners can assess the performance of their own top management only by a relatively general comparison with other similar firms and with the stock market as a whole.

The ignorance of stockholders drastically reduces the amount of marginal switching they do from one stock to another that appears to be enjoying better performance. They simply cannot accurately judge small differences in quality of performance. Moreover, the capital gains tax "rakes off" 25 per cent of all value appreciation every time a stockholder switches from one stock to another. Thus the force of competition among different stocks, which would in theory be expected to put pressure on top management to *maximize* the rate of growth of its stock price, is in fact severely weakened by both ignorance and the tax structure.

As a result, owners tend to act as "satisficers" instead of "maximizers." *In our interpretation "satisficers" differ from "maximizers" only in capability, not in intention.* They would like to maximize, but the limitations of their ignorance and their finite capacity cause them to adopt behavior different from that of a theoretical maximizer. Consequently, if the price increases of the firm's stock meet some minimal criterion of "satisfactory growth" in comparison with alternative investments, and dividends do not fall, they will approve of the firm's top management. If the performance of the firm is so poor that these results are clearly not being attained, they will disapprove of the firm's top management.

Owners express their approval or disapproval of managers in the annual elections of the board of directors. However, because of the diffusion of ownership, it takes an extraordinarily poor management performance to trigger a real uprising among stockholders—an uprising violent enough to elect directors who will remove or drastically discipline the top managers. Normally, top management controls the board of directors through proxy agreements; hence the key executives are self-perpetuating unless they radically disappoint the owners.

Nevertheless, fear of potential rebellion among stockholders imposes a latent check on the actions of the incumbent management. This fear is increased by the operations of professional "outside raiders" who specialize in rallying dissident owners against incumbent managers. The New York Central Railroad over the years has provided a number of examples of revolts sparked by such "outsiders."

Moreover, although a very poor management performance may result in a rebellion, a very good one does not usually cause a powerful movement among stockholders to reward their managers

with lavish bonuses. Hence *the punishment for grievous error is greater than the reward for outstanding success.* This asymmetry between failure and success tends to make the managers of a diffused-ownership firm behave differently from the managers of the type of owner-managed firm envisioned by traditional theory.

Although a majority of stock owners in the United States seek "safe growth" as described above, a certain minority are far more interested in rapid appreciation of stock prices. They are the buyers of so-called growth stocks. However, we are excluding these owners from our analysis because (1) Most of the large corporations in the United States with widely diffused ownership are not "growth" corporations. But our theory applies only to diffused-ownership firms. (2) "Growth" stocks comprise a small minority of all stocks (although they receive a great deal of publicity).

D. THE MOTIVATION OF MANAGERS

Our second central hypothesis is simply the application of self-interest to the managers of large firms. Today the largest, most significant firms in the United States are owned by thousands of individual stockholders who are remote from actual management and decision-making. Conversely, the men who really run these firms are professional managers. Although they may own some stock, their ownership is usually a *result* of their executive positions, rather than the *cause* of their holding such positions. Also, their incomes are not identical with the firm's profits, and may not even vary in any strict relation to the firm's profits. As a result, when managers act in their own self-interest, they do not always act in the interest of the owners.[6]

[6] See Baumol, *op. cit.*

What *is* in their self-interest is maximizing *their own* incomes. As prudent men, they consider their (discounted) incomes over the course of their *entire working lives*, not just in the current year, or while working for their current employer. These incomes include both *monetary elements* (salaries, bonuses, capital gains from stock options, etc.) and *non-monetary elements* (leisure, prestige, power, etc.).[7] The non-monetary aspects of income can be equated at the margin with dollars; hence we can conceive of the managers as maximizing the present value of their lifetime incomes in dollar terms.

The pursuit of self-interest by managers also has important repercussions upon relationships *among managers* within the firm itself. Just as it is not always in the interest of top management to maximize the returns to the owners, it may not always be in the interest of the middle management to carry out the orders of top management. It is necessary, therefore, to break the firm down into its component parts in order to discover the levels on which individual motivations actually operate.

It should be pointed out that the self-interest of individual managers has definite limits. We certainly do not mean to depict corporate managers as avaricious, grasping individuals willing to break every moral law in their ruthless drive to success—as the jackets of some business novels have put it. We do not impute any more self-interest to managers as a group than to the members of other social or economic groups. We merely assume that an important fraction of all managers is sufficiently motivated by

[7] Our definition of managerial *income* is thus operationally similar to Williamson's definition of managerial *utility*; hence our income-maximizing assumption is akin to his utility-maximizing assumption (see Williamson, *op. cit.*, chap. iii).

self-interest to count its own long-run welfare as more important than the welfare of either the owners of the firm or the other managers therein.

IV. IMPACT OF BUREAUCRACY ON BEHAVIOR OF FIRMS

In order to analyze in more detail the way in which managers in very large firms make decisions, it is first necessary to examine the *context* of managerial decision-making. Each manager occupies a certain position in the organizational pyramid formed by the corporate hierarchy. Above him are his *superiors*, who have control over his promotions, salary, bonuses, and other elements of his success. Below him are his *subordinates*, whose promotions and income he analogously influences and whose efforts he depends upon to produce results pleasing to his superiors. Alongside him at other positions on the same level of the hierarchy are his *peers*. They are engaged in specialized tasks different from his own, but they are competing with him for eventual promotion to higher levels. *The basic problem which each manager faces is the necessity of pleasing his superior to attain advances in income* (either through promotion to higher-paying jobs or a higher salary in his existing job). In the case of top management, the superiors involved are represented by the board of directors and the stockholders.

From the point of view of each firm's owners, the function of managers and employees is to make the greatest possible contribution toward achieving the objectives of the owners. But whatever the owners' objectives may be, we believe that *the bureaucratic structure of large firms will cause management to deviate systematically from achieving ownership objectives*. This will occur because (1) the motives of managers are not identical with the motives of owners, as we have pointed out, and (2) in large companies, the nature of the administrative structure makes it impossible for the owners to control the behavior of managers completely—or even for top managers to control the behavior of those below them completely.

The following specific factors may cause managerial behavior to deviate from ownership objectives:

1. It is often very difficult to measure accurately the contribution made by each individual employee to profits, stock-price gains, or any other financial objectives. In such instances —which may cover a majority of management personnel in a large corporation—superiors are driven to use subjective impressions or irrelevant objective tests they have set up as means of deciding whom to promote. Therefore they must promote men who somehow make the most favorable impression on them, and these may not necessarily be the men who actually contribute most to ownership (or top management) objectives.

2. The superiors themselves may not be pursuing policies which are identical with those of the firm's owners. If so, they might tend to promote men who carried out the policies they were pursuing rather than men who carried out policies which maximized the owners' objectives.

Insofar as either of the above factors is in effect, managers on the middle and lower levels of the corporate bureaucracy will find themselves best served by actions which create the most favorable impression upon their superiors, regardless of the impact of such actions upon corporate profits or other ownership gains. Of course, the subjective impressions of their superiors will by no means be divorced entirely from factual evidence; hence no manager can completely ignore the possible objectively measurable effects of his behavior upon corporate prosperity. But the tools which measure individual contributions to profits or stock-price increases are often very imprecise, especially regarding such non-selling and non-production jobs as public relations, personnel management, and advertising. Therefore an individual manager may be able to choose among several alternative actions which will affect profits or stock prices in the long run, but which will have no differing effects upon the objective indexes which his superiors must rely on to rate the quality of his performance. If a number of executives in a firm select among such policies so as to please their superiors rather than to maximize ownership objectives, the cumulative effect of such choices may in the long run cause a substantial loss of potential benefits to the firm's owners.

Even more important are the long-run effects of certain actions managers may take to advance their own interests which reduce the firm's efficiency. Since the managers are motivated by the advancement of their own incomes, they will perform acts which impair the firm's efficiency if (1) those acts tend to advance their own interests, and (2) it is impossible or very difficult for their superiors to discover these acts. Gordon Tullock has presented an ingenious and persuasive theory of political bureaucracies which encompasses a number of such actions.[8] Among those applicable to corporate bureaucracies are the following:

1. *Managers at every level of the corporate pyramid tend to screen information in their possession so that only data favorable to them are passed upward to their superiors.* Insofar as cost accounting and other auditing techniques administered by outsiders are available to the su-

[8] "A General Theory of Politics" (undated and unpublished mimeographed manuscript).

periors, this cannot be done. But there is always a considerable element of judgment in information flowing through the corporate hierarchy. Hence managers can screen out judgment factors unfavorable to them before they pass data upward to those who have authority over their own incomes and appurtenances. Also, in order to please superiors, managers may tend to pass to them only information that verifies the desires of the superiors, or proves that their decisions were wise.

If the corporate hierarchy has many levels, the cumulative effect of this screening process may become substantial. For example, assume that the top level of a corporation is designated the A level, the next level, the B level, etc. and that there are five levels in all. Each A executive has a number of B-level men (say, three) under him; each B executive has a similar group of C-level men under him; and so on, down to the lowest or E-level, which consists of men "in the field" who receive information "first hand." In theory, each man passes on information to his superior, who winnows the most important data from the many reports made to him and passes those upward to *his* superior. This process is repeated up to the A level, where the top men make decisions based on the information emerging from the hierarchy below them. Thus, screening information is a legitimate part of each manager's job. But he may deliberately (or even unconsciously) suppress some of the information which his superiors need to know because that information is either unfavorable to himself or displeasing to his superiors. If each manager thus suppresses only 10 per cent of the data he should pass upward if top management is to be properly informed, then managers at the A level will receive only 66

per cent of the important data fed into the pyramid at the E level ($0.9^4 = 0.656$).

Thus the tendency for managers to screen information may cause top management to be systematically misinformed through (*a*) failure to learn vital facts, especially ones adverse to lower management levels, and (*b*) a tendency to be told only what they want to hear.

2. *Managers at every level tend to carry out only part of the orders given to them.* Since the personnel of each corporation are pursuing their own interests instead of the firm's, they will be reluctant to carry out any orders which would reduce their income, power, prestige, or chances of advancement. To some extent, they must obey such orders because they will be fired for insubordination if they flatly refuse. However, the vigor with which they execute such policies, their attention to proper follow-up procedures, and their imaginative application of these policies in new situations may be minimized without any actual insubordination. The technique of "kicking it around until it disappears" is well known in all large organizations.

The cumulative effects of such partial failure to execute orders can be very great if a corporation has many layers in its organization hierarchy. In the case of the five-level organization cited above, a failure by each layer of managers below level A to carry out just 5 per cent of the orders they receive from their superiors would result in only 81 per cent of the top management's orders being carried out by the lowest level personnel ($0.95^4 = 0.814$). Moreover, some allowance must also be made for inefficiency in carrying out orders due to incompetence, inertia, and misunderstanding.

It is true that cost accounting, auditing, and other objective performance reports can significantly reduce the abil-

ity of subordinates to practice unde-
tected insubordination. Nevertheless, no
large corporation actually carries out the
policies established by its leaders in precisely the manner originally envisioned
by those leaders.

We realize that there are many techniques that owners and top managers
can use to counteract the above inefficiencies. Corporate spies, peer-group
pressures, personal ties between members
of top management and lower management, random inspections, and a host of
other devices are often used to produce
closer conformance of subordinates' behavior to the desires and policies of owners and top managers. Nevertheless, we
believe that all of these remedies are only
partially successful in very large organizations. As a result, the inefficiencies described above cause large firms to deviate systematically and significantly from
the course of action that would in fact
maximize attainment of the owners'
objectives—or even the objectives of top
management.

These inefficiencies are inherent in all
large organizations. Hence they will exist
not only in large managerial firms with
diffused ownership, but also in large non-
profit organizations, large owner-managed firms, and even large government
agencies. Therefore, even if we agreed
with traditional theory that the owners
of a firm wish to maximize profits (and
we do agree in the case of owner-managed firms), we would contend that the
difference between *owner* motivation and
managerial motivation will cause systematic deviations from profit-maximizing behavior as long as the firm is large
enough so that the owners themselves
cannot supervise all facets of its activities.

When such large size exists, the owners must yield some discretion over the
firm's behavior to managers whose goals
are not identical with the goals of the
owners. The manager at the top of a large
firm, or the owner in a profit-maximizing
firm, must delegate authority to others
(that is, permit the screening of information and give some discretion to his subordinates in carrying out his orders) because his own personal *capacity* to handle
information and decisions is limited at a
level below the amount of information
and problems generated by the organization. This is a function of *size*. However
it does not *necessarily* create inefficiency.
Inefficiency arises whenever such delegation of authority leads to results other
than those which are optimal from the
viewpoint of the top man. But non-
optimal results may occur because the
goals of the persons to whom he has
delegated authority are different from his
own. If these subordinates had goals precisely identical to his own, then they
would act as mechanical extensions of his
own capacity. That is the implicit assumption of the classical literature on the
firm to which we object.

Thus, in essence, some behavior which
is non-optimal from the viewpoint of the
top man arises because of *both* size and
goal divergence. Large size is what requires him to delegate authority in the
first place; but goal divergence can cause
that delegation to create non-optimal
results.

Even if the top man had subordinates
whose goals were exactly identical to his
own, some inefficiencies of a *technical* nature might arise, again due to the limited
capacity of each individual decision-
maker in the firm. For example, specialists working in different parts of the firm
whose activities had unforeseen overlapping effects might not realize this fact
until some unco-ordinated behavior had
taken place; that is, until the behavior of

one somehow impeded the plans of the other, unbeknown to the first. This kind of inefficiency is due *entirely* to the size of the firm; that is, to the fact that individuals have limited capacities and the firm is larger than their capacities. But behavior of the firm which is not optimal from the viewpoint of the top man can be caused *either* by size alone (technical inefficiency) or by a combination of size and divergent goals (technical plus motivational inefficiency). Screening, of course, arises because of size. But screening per se is not necessarily a form of inefficiency. It can lead to inefficiency without any difference in motives, but it does not *always* lead to inefficiency *unless* a difference of motives is also present. Then screening will always create inefficiency to some extent.

V. IMPLICATIONS OF THE THEORY REGARDING BEHAVIOR OF MANAGEMENT

Now that we have set forth our basic theory and examined the bureaucratic context of managerial decision-making, we will explore the theory's implications regarding the behavior of managers at various levels within the firm.

A. TOP-MANAGEMENT BEHAVIOR

1. *The organizational setting.*—The top managers in a large firm are those few key executives who are involved in making basic policy and planning decisions. They are normally paid for their performance in three ways: (*a*) by salaries and bonuses, (*b*) by stock options, and (*c*) by expense accounts and other untaxed perquisites. However, high personal income-tax rates limit the amount of their salaries and bonuses they can retain, and they cannot *retain* any wealth from expense accounts and other similar untaxed benefits. Therefore, top managers

normally regard stock options as a very significant form of compensation. Hence, top management normally has a direct and powerful interest in the *market price* of the firm's stock. Clearly, creation of such an interest is the primary justification of the stock-option arrangement from the owners' point of view, although the nature and size of the arrangement is usually determined by the managers themselves.

An important part of top management's environment consists of groups outside the firm's administrative structure who are in a position to challenge the quality of top management's performance. They include labor unions, government officials, and the public at large. Strong criticism from any of these groups can seriously tarnish the general public image of all-around competence which top management seeks to foster by "getting along well" with all important groups. This type of public image is far more significant to top management in a concentrated-ownership firm. When more significant to top management in a diffused-ownership firm than in an owner-managed firm or a concentrated-ownership firm. When ownership is diffused among thousands of stockholders, the owners are almost indistinguishable from the general public insofar as top management is concerned; hence the public image of the firm is very likely to be the owners' image too. Moreover, stockholders have so few contacts with management that any widely circulated criticism of top management is likely to convince many stockholders that "where there's smoke, there's fire." Therefore, top management is often highly sensitive to criticism from major groups outside the firm.

2. *Top management's promotional strategy.*—The best way for top man-

agement to maximize its own lifetime income is to "keep the stockholders happy." This normally involves three basic policies:

a) *Carefully screening all information which is forwarded to stockholders or the public at large* so that it reflects an outstanding management performance. The results of this policy can be readily seen by reading a typical annual report or attending an annual stockholders' meeting. Of course, professional reporting agencies like the *Wall Street Journal* provide some objective check on management's ability to suppress unfavorable information. However, it is quite easy for managers to conceal a great deal of inefficiency from such "outsiders," especially since only outstanding blunders make good news copy.

b) *Directing the firm toward achievement of constant or slightly rising dividends plus steadily increasing stock prices.* However, top management need only attain a "satisfactory" rate of stock-price growth, not a "maximum" one.

c) *Maintaining a "public image" of competence by avoiding controversy and criticism.* Public criticism of the firm or controversy about its policies tends to contradict this "image" and raise doubts in the minds of the stockholders about the wisdom of retaining the existing top management.

3. *Implications of top-management behavior.*—The result of top management's employing the above policies is that the firm (a) is more likely to avoid risky decisions, (b) will have less variability of earnings, (c) may grow more slowly, and (d) will be less likely to go bankrupt than it would if the managers sought to maximize profits. Top management will avoid highly risky decisions because they might cause the earnings of the firm to fluctuate instead of growing steadily,

even if the total profits of the firm would be larger with fluctuating earnings. Top management abhors fluctuating earnings for the following reasons:

a) If the earnings in a given year decline, the price of the stock may fall. This would be repugnant to all owners—including the top managers themselves—and might cause the owners to throw out top management, especially if the stock market in general has risen.

b) Stocks with fluctuating earnings generally have lower price-earnings ratios than those with steadily rising earnings. It is clearly in the interest of all owners—including top managers with stock options—to maintain high price-earnings ratios.

Thus the attention of management is focused on stock *prices* rather than *earnings* (profits), which are viewed as means to obtain higher stock prices rather than as ends in themselves. Therefore, if top management must choose between (a) maximizing profits over a given period by accepting fluctuating earnings, or (b) achieving total profits by maintaining steadily rising annual earnings, it will normally choose the latter. Therefore, diffused-ownership firms will experience less *variability of earnings* than firms which try to maximize profits.

In our opinion, this relatively conservative attitude by top management would lead to slower growth than a "pure" policy of profit maximization *among those firms which survive.* Other implications of our hypothesis and forecasts consistent with it concerning top management behavior are as follows:

a) Research and development expenditures are more likely to be budgeted for steady yearly growth than for "crash" expansion of promising innovations.

b) Diffused-ownership firms will exhibit a strong predilection for diversification of products, especially through merger, as a means of reducing risks taken on any one product or line of products. Since diversification through merger tends to reduce the rate of return on capital, owner-managers would be less likely to adopt such policies.

c) Financing rapid expansion through additional stock offerings is less likely to be used by top management in diffused-ownership firms than by owner-managers. In many cases, the original owners of a firm which expands rapidly use sales of common stock to "buy themselves out" of the corporation, thus capitalizing on their original ownership interest. Managers whose only stock comes from stock options are more likely to adopt internal financing, bank borrowing, or bond issues for such financing so as not to dilute their own interests. Among long-established firms, both owner-managed and managerial types will probably avoid additional equity financing with equal distaste because of its dilution effects. However, managers may be willing to finance through stock offerings if they feel that the additional capital will enable the firm to rapidly expand sales. The work of McGuire, Chiu, and Elbing has shown that executive incomes are significantly correlated to firm sales.[9] Under the above circumstances, then, professional management will have to decide which course of action will most likely maximize their life time incomes—raising less capital from internal financing or obtaining greater financing (and stock dilution) from stock offerings.

d) Top management will be much more sensitive to public, union, and government criticism than owner-managers

[9] J. W. McGuire, J. S. Y. Chiu, and A. O. Elbing, "Executive Incomes, Sales and Profits," *American Economic Review*, September, 1962.

would be. Hence top managers will be more conciliatory in their public dealings than might be required for profit maximization.

e) Top managers will use their roles in the firm to enhance their own personal prestige and stature. As a result, they will contribute to local causes and participate in community affairs more than they should from a purely profit-maximizing point of view.

f) In order to stabilize future profits, avoid controversy, and prevent adverse publicity, top management may make concessions to labor unions more readily than owner-managers would. This will tend to reduce profits below the level which would be attained by a truly profit-maximizing firm.

g) Expense accounts are likely to be more extravagant in managerial firms than they would be if managers really maximized returns to owners. Although expense-account benefits and salaries are both deductible, salaries are a much more visible and easily checked form of management compensation. Therefore, managers will seek to expand expense-account benefits in order to raise their total compensation without attracting the attention of owners. This will result in greater total compensation for them than is required to retain their services. The fact that such non-salary benefits will influence their choices among firms (and hence may appear to be a necessary part of their compensation by each firm) does not destroy this argument. Managers *as a group* are probably extracting rent because of inflated expense accounts; that is, they are compensated more in *all* managerial firms than is necessary to keep them from becoming non-managers. Thus what may appear as true costs to individual firms are still an excessive reduction of profits among all managerial firms compared with what profits would be if truly maximized.

h) Managerial firms are likely to respond more slowly to declines in profits than they would if they really pursued profit maximization. Since managers wish to preserve their personal prerogatives (such as large expense accounts) and do not suffer directly from lower profits, they will be willing to "ride out" a sudden decline in profits without cutting back expenditures in the hope that it will be temporary. In contrast, true profit-maximizers would exhibit no such inertia but would immediately alter their existing behavior patterns. However, if lower profits continue, even managerial firms will adjust their behavior so as to avoid having lower yearly earnings cause any decline in stock prices (if possible).

B. MIDDLE-MANAGEMENT BEHAVIOR

1. *The organizational setting.*—Middle managers are those operating executives under top management who are responsible for carrying out various specialized tasks within the firm. Middle managers are normally paid for their performance primarily by salaries and bonuses and secondarily by expense accounts and other untaxed perquisites.

2. *Middle management's promotional strategy.*—The best way for middle managers to maximize their lifetime incomes is to increase the size of those incomes by being promoted to higher-paying positions within the firm or in other firms. Since their promotions are determined by the recommendations of their superiors, their efforts to obtain promotion consist essentially of doing whatever will most please and impress their superiors, regardless of the effects of their actions upon the profits of the firm.

We have already pointed out several

ways in which this type of motivation will cause deviations from "pure" profit maximization. In addition, middle managers must get along well with their subordinates, since they must rely upon the performance of the latter to assist them in impressing top management. This dual need for pleasing superiors and co-operating with subordinates places middle managers in a somewhat different position from top managers. Top management can employ cost accounting, personal ties with lower management, peer-group informants, and numerous other devices to keep well-informed about what middle managers are doing. This means that middle managers have much less scope for covering up mistakes than do top managers—even though the magnitude of the errors which top managers might make is much greater.

3. *Implications of middle-management behavior.*—Middle managers will normally tend to be risk-avoiders in making decisions. A certain degree of advancement can be obtained merely by surviving, doing daily tasks, and not committing any outstanding blunders. This tendency, plus the desire of middle management to initiate those ideas which reflect the preconceived notions of their superiors, may produce an excessive lack of creativity and innovation at the middle-management level. Consequently, the firm may pass by many profit-increasing possibilities on the middle-management level which would be taken up by a truly profit-maximizing firm.

Insofar as middle managers are intrusted with labor relations, they may also tend to grant concessions to unions more readily than owner-managers would. Since strikes always involve more risks due to uncertainty than do settlements, risk-avoiders will have a built-in bias toward achieving settlements through concessions. Again, the result may be lower profits than would be attained by more aggressive and tougher owner-manager firms.

In highly decentralized firms, middle managers may be intrusted with far more responsibility than in centralized firms. In such cases, middle managers will undertake much riskier actions because the potential rewards will be higher. In fact, the position of middle management in such firms is riskier than the position of top management, because, as noted, middle managers are more closely scrutinized by their superiors than are top managers. Thus the attitude of middle managers toward risks depends largely upon the structure of costs and rewards associated with different types of behavior on their part. The middle managers at General Electric and Westinghouse involved in price-fixing litigation were apparently willing to take on extraordinary risks in order to gain entry into the ranks of top management.

C. LOWER-MANAGEMENT BEHAVIOR

1. *The organizational setting.*—Lower managers are those supervisory personnel at the foreman or comparable level who have direct authority over production or lowest-level clerical personnel. They are normally paid for their performance by salaries and bonuses. Their salaries are partly based on seniority and longevity in the firm, and their bonuses are based on achieving production or quality goals. Normally, lower managers have little expectation of being promoted in middle or top management because the educational standards for those higher echelons are beyond their capabilities.

2. *Lower management's promotional strategy.*—The best way for lower man-

agers to maximize their lifetime incomes is to seek promotions up to the highest attainable lower-management level and then to hold on to what they have achieved. Often their performances can be accurately measured objectively by means of production quotas, quality checks, costs accounting, etc. Thus the efforts of lower management are more intensively directed at meeting objective performance criteria than is the case with middle and top management.

3. *Implications of lower-management behavior.*—Lower managers are risk-avoiders of a high order. Their aim is primarily to retain their present positions by meeting quotas and avoiding gross errors. In this echelon are the classic bureaucrats who never violate the rules and fear to "stick their necks out." As with middle management, the result is undoubtedly a lower level of creativity, innovation, and risk-taking than would occur in a firm perfectly organized to maximize profits.

D. NON-MANAGEMENT PERSONNEL:
THE WORKERS

In our analysis of the firm into several parts, we have deliberately ignored those workers who are not part of the firm's management structure. They are normally distinguished from management personnel because they are paid hourly rates instead of salaries. In most large, diffused-ownership firms, these workers are members of labor unions which represent them in collective bargaining with management. It is already a well-accepted tenet in economic theory that union leaders and members are not motivated by profit maximization for the firm which employs them. For this reason, we believe that unionized workers (and perhaps even non-unionized workers) should be considered as factors of production hired by the firm rather than constituent parts of it.

VI. SUMMARY

1. We have proposed a modified theory of the firm to explain the behavior of large, diffused-ownership firms, which we refer to as *large managerial* firms. This theory assumes that ownership and management are essentially separate, and that each such firm is so large that its management hierarchy contains at least three types of managers: top, middle, and lower. We postulate that both owners and managers act in their own self-interest by pursuing the following goals:

a) Owners are basically *satisficers* who desire uninterrupted dividends and a steady rise in the price of the firm's stock. Their remoteness from the firm's actual affairs makes it impossible for them to press for profit-maximizing behavior.

b) Managers are "economic men" who *desire to maximize their own lifetime incomes* (which includes both monetary and non-monetary elements), principally by obtaining rapid promotions as a result of pleasing their superiors in the firm.

2. The behavior of large managerial firms deviates from the profit maximization posited by the traditional theory of the firm for the following reasons:

a) The large size of such firms requires them to develop *bureaucratic management* structures which cannot be perfectly controlled by the men in charge of them. In particular, these structures tend to (i) provide biased information to top management which reflects its own desires and ideas too strongly and (ii) only partially carry out the orders issued by top management. These tendencies cause systematic deviations from what-

ever goals the organization is ostensibly pursuing. They exist in large owner-managed firms as well as large managerial firms, since they result from sheer size. In essence, such deviations are caused by divergences of goals *within* management; that is, between middle and lower management on the one hand and top management on the other. These goal divergences are able to influence the firm's behavior because large size both compels top managers to delegate authority to their subordinates and prevents them from checking up completely on how that authority is used. This behavior of the firm which is not optimal from the viewpoint of the top man can be caused *either* by size alone (technical inefficiency) or by a combination of size and divergent goals (technical plus motivational inefficiency).

b) The separation of ownership and management limits owners to being satisficers instead of maximizers; hence managers aim at achieving steady growth of earnings plus gradually rising stock prices instead of maximum profits. As a result, large managerial firms are more cautious; spend less on "crash" research programs; experience less variability of profits; have larger expense accounts; evidence more conciliation in dealings with government, unions, and the public; and probably grow more slowly than they would if they sought to maximize profits. In essence, these outcomes result from the divergence of goals *between* owners and top management set forth in paragraph 1 above. The size and structure of the firm both compel owners to delegate authority to top management and prevent them from checking up fully on its performance or imposing their own goals upon top management.

[6]

Up and down with ecology— the "issue-attention cycle"

ANTHONY DOWNS

AMERICAN public attention rarely remains sharply focused upon any one domestic issue for very long—even if it involves a continuing problem of crucial importance to society. Instead, a systematic "issue-attention cycle" seems strongly to influence public attitudes and behavior concerning most key domestic problems. Each of these problems suddenly leaps into prominence, remains there for a short time, and then—though still largely unresolved—gradually fades from the center of public attention. A study of the way this cycle operates provides insights into how long public attention is likely to remain sufficiently focused upon any given issue to generate enough political pressure to cause effective change.

The shaping of American attitudes toward improving the quality of our environment provides both an example and a potential test of this "issue-attention cycle." In the past few years, there has been a remarkably widespread upsurge of interest in the quality of our environment. This change in public attitudes has been much faster than any changes in the environment itself. What has caused this shift in public attention? Why did this issue suddenly assume so high a priority among our domestic concerns? And how long will the American public sustain high-intensity interest in ecological matters? I believe that answers to these questions can be derived from analyzing the "issue-attention cycle."

The dynamics of the "issue-attention cycle"

Public perception of most "crises" in American domestic life does not reflect changes in real conditions as much as it reflects the operation of a systematic cycle of heightening public interest and then increasing boredom with major issues. This "issue-attention cycle" is rooted both in the nature of certain domestic problems and in the way major communications media interact with the public. The cycle itself has five stages, which may vary in duration depending upon the particular issue involved, but which almost always occur in the following sequence:

1. **The pre-problem stage.** This prevails when some highly undesirable social condition exists but has not yet captured much public attention, even though some experts or interest groups may already be alarmed by it. *Usually, objective conditions regarding the problem are far worse during the pre-problem stage than they are by the time the public becomes interested in it.* For example, this was true of racism, poverty, and malnutrition in the United States.

2. **Alarmed discovery and euphoric enthusiasm.** As a result of some dramatic series of events (like the ghetto riots in 1965 to 1967), or for other reasons, the public suddenly becomes both aware of and alarmed about the evils of a particular problem. This alarmed discovery is invariably accompanied by euphoric enthusiasm about society's ability to "solve this problem" or "do something effective" within a relatively short time. The combination of alarm and confidence results in part from the strong public pressure in America for political leaders to claim that every problem can be "solved." This outlook is rooted in the great American tradition of optimistically viewing most obstacles to social progress as *external* to the structure of society itself. The implication is that every obstacle can be eliminated and every problem solved *without any fundamental reordering of society itself*, if only we devote sufficient effort to it. In older and perhaps wiser cultures, there is an underlying sense of irony or even pessimism which springs from a widespread and often confirmed belief that many problems cannot be "solved" *at all* in any complete sense. Only recently has this more pessimistic view begun to develop in our culture.

3. **Realizing the cost of significant progress.** The third stage consists of a gradually spreading realization that the cost of "solving" the

problem is very high indeed. Really doing so would not only take
a great deal of money but would also require major sacrifices by
large groups in the population. The public thus begins to realize that
part of the problem results from arrangements that are providing
significant benefits to someone—often to millions. For example, traffic
congestion and a great deal of smog are caused by increasing automobile usage. Yet this also enhances the mobility of millions of Americans who continue to purchase more vehicles to obtain these
advantages.

In certain cases, technological progress can eliminate some of the
undesirable results of a problem without causing any major restructuring of society or any loss of present benefits by others (except
for higher money costs). In the optimistic American tradition, such
a technological solution is initially assumed to be possible in the case
of nearly every problem. Our most pressing social problems, however, usually involve either deliberate or unconscious exploitation
of one group in society by another, or the prevention of one group
from enjoying something that others want to keep for themselves.
For example, most upper-middle-class whites value geographic separation from poor people and blacks. Hence any equality of access to
the advantages of suburban living for the poor and for blacks cannot
be achieved without some sacrifice by middle-class whites of the
"benefits" of separation. The increasing recognition that there is this
type of relationship between the problem and its "solution" constitutes a key part of the third stage.

4. **Gradual decline of intense public interest.** The previous stage becomes almost imperceptibly transformed into the fourth stage: a
gradual decline in the intensity of public interest in the problem. As
more and more people realize how difficult, and how costly to themselves, a solution to the problem would be, three reactions set in.
Some people just get discouraged. Others feel positively threatened
by thinking about the problem; so they suppress such thoughts. Still
others become bored by the issue. Most people experience some
combination of these feelings. Consequently, public desire to keep
attention focused on the issue wanes. And by this time, some other
issue is usually entering Stage Two; so it exerts a more novel and thus
more powerful claim upon public attention.

5. **The post-problem stage.** In the final stage, an issue that has been
replaced at the center of public concern moves into a prolonged
limbo—a twilight realm of lesser attention or spasmodic recurrences
of interest. However, the issue now has a different relation to public
attention than that which prevailed in the "pre-problem" stage. For

one thing, during the time that interest was sharply focused on this problem, new institutions, programs, and policies may have been created to help solve it. These entities almost always persist and often have some impact even after public attention has shifted elsewhere. For example, during the early stages of the "War on Poverty," the Office of Economic Opportunity (OEO) was established, and it initiated many new programs. Although poverty has now faded as a central public issue, OEO still exists. Moreover, many of its programs have experienced significant success, even though funded at a far lower level than would be necessary to reduce poverty decisively.

Any major problem that once was elevated to national prominence may sporadically recapture public interest; or important aspects of it may become attached to some other problem that subsequently dominates center stage. Therefore, problems that have gone through the cycle almost always receive a higher average level of attention, public effort, and general concern than those still in the pre-discovery stage.

Which problems are likely to go through the cycle?

Not all major social problems go through this "issue-attention cycle." Those which do generally possess to some degree three specific characteristics. First, the majority of persons in society are not suffering from the problem nearly as much as some minority (a *numerical* minority, not necessarily an *ethnic* one). This is true of many pressing social problems in America today—poverty, racism, poor public transportation, low-quality education, crime, drug addiction, and unemployment, among others. The number of persons suffering from each of these ills is very large *absolutely*—in the millions. But the numbers are small *relatively*—usually less than 15 per cent of the entire population. Therefore, most people do not suffer directly enough from such problems to keep their attention riveted on them.

Second, the sufferings caused by the problem are generated by social arrangements that provide significant benefits to a majority or a powerful minority of the population. For example, Americans who own cars—plus the powerful automobile and highway lobbies —receive short-run benefits from the prohibition of using motor-fuel tax revenues for financing public transportation systems, even though such systems are desperately needed by the urban poor.

Third, the problem has no intrinsically exciting qualities—or no longer has them. When big-city racial riots were being shown nightly on the nation's television screens, public attention naturally focused upon their causes and consequences. But when they ceased (or at least the media stopped reporting them so intensively), public interest in the problems related to them declined sharply. Similarly, as long as the National Aeronautics and Space Administration (NASA) was able to stage a series of ever more thrilling space shots, culminating in the worldwide television spectacular of Americans walking on the moon, it generated sufficient public support to sustain high-level Congressional appropriations. But NASA had nothing half so dramatic for an encore, and repetition of the same feat proved less and less exciting (though a near disaster on the third try did revive audience interest). So NASA's Congressional appropriations plummeted.

A problem must be dramatic and exciting to maintain public interest because news is "consumed" by much of the American public (and by publics everywhere) largely as a form of entertainment. As such, it competes with other types of entertainment for a share of each person's time. Every day, there is a fierce struggle for space in the highly limited universe of newsprint and television viewing time. Each issue vies not only with all other social problems and public events, but also with a multitude of "non-news" items that are often far more pleasant to contemplate. These include sporting news, weather reports, crossword puzzles, fashion accounts, comics, and daily horoscopes. In fact, the amount of television time and newspaper space devoted to sports coverage, as compared to international events, is a striking commentary on the relative value that the public places on knowing about these two subjects.

When all three of the above conditions exist concerning a given problem that has somehow captured public attention, the odds are great that it will soon move through the entire "issue-attention cycle" —and therefore will gradually fade from the center of the stage. The first condition means that most people will not be continually reminded of the problem by their own suffering from it. The second condition means that solving the problem requires sustained attention and effort, plus fundamental changes in social institutions or behavior. This in turn means that significant attempts to solve it are threatening to important groups in society. The third condition means that the media's sustained focus on this problem soon bores a majority of the public. As soon as the media realize that their emphasis on this problem is threatening many people and boring even more, they will shift their focus to some "new" problem. This is particularly likely in America because nearly all the media are run for profit, and they make the most money by appealing to the largest possible audiences. Thus, as Marshall McLuhan has pointed out, it is largely the audience itself—the American public—that "manages the news" by maintaining or losing interest in a given subject. As long as this pattern persists, we will continue to be confronted by a stream of "crises" involving particular social problems. Each will rise into public view, capture center stage for a while, and then gradually fade away as it is replaced by more fashionable issues moving into their "crisis" phases.

The rise of environmental concern

Public interest in the quality of the environment now appears to be about midway through the "issue-attention cycle." Gradually, more and more people are beginning to realize the immensity of the social and financial costs of cleaning up our air and water and of preserving and restoring open spaces. Hence much of the enthusiasm about prompt, dramatic improvement in the environment is fading. There is still a great deal of public interest, however, so it cannot be said that the "post-problem stage" has been reached. In fact, as will be discussed later, the environmental issue may well retain more attention than social problems that affect smaller proportions of the population. Before evaluating the prospects of long-term interest in the environment, though, it is helpful to analyze how environmental concern passed through the earlier stages in the "issue-attention cycle."

The most obvious reason for the initial rise in concern about the environment is the recent deterioration of certain easily perceived environmental conditions. A whole catalogue of symptoms can be arrayed, including ubiquitous urban smog, greater proliferation of solid waste, oceanic oil spills, greater pollution of water supplies by DDT and other poisons, the threatened disappearance of many wildlife species, and the overcrowding of a variety of facilities from commuter expressways to National Parks. Millions of citizens observing these worsening conditions became convinced that *someone* ought to "do something" about them. But "doing something" to reduce environmental deterioration is not easy. For many of our environmental problems have been caused by developments which are highly valued by most Americans.

The very abundance of our production and consumption of material goods is responsible for an immense amount of environmental pollution. For example, electric power generation, if based on fossil fuels, creates smoke and air pollution or, if based on nuclear fuels, causes rising water temperatures. Yet a key foundation for rising living standards in the United States during this century has been the doubling of electric power consumption every 10 years. So more pollution is the price we have paid for the tremendous advantages of being able to use more and more electricity. Similarly, much of the litter blighting even our remotest landscapes stems from the convenience of using "throwaway packages." Thus, to regard environmental pollution as a purely external negative factor would be to ignore its direct linkage with material advantages most citizens enjoy.

Another otherwise favorable development that has led to rising environmental pollution is what I would call the democratization of privilege. Many more Americans are now able to participate in certain activities that were formerly available only to a small, wealthy minority. Some members of that minority are incensed by the consequences of having their formerly esoteric advantages spread to "the common man." The most frequent irritant caused by the democratization of privilege is congestion. Rising highway congestion, for example, is denounced almost everywhere. Yet its main cause is the rapid spread of automobile ownership and usage. In 1950, about 59 per cent of all families had at least one automobile, and seven per cent owned two or more. By 1968, the proportion of families owning at least one automobile had climbed to 79 per cent, and 26 per cent had two or more cars. In the 10 years from 1960 to 1970, the total number of registered automotive vehicles rose by 35 million (or 47 per cent), as compared to a rise in human population of 23 million (or only 13 per cent). Moreover, it has been estimated that motor vehicles cause approximately 60 per cent of all air pollution. So the tremendous increase in smog does not result primarily from larger population, but rather from the democratization of automobile ownership.

The democratization of privilege also causes crowding in National Parks, rising suburban housing density, the expansion of new subdivisions into formerly picturesque farms and orchards, and the transformation of once tranquil resort areas like Waikiki Beach into forests of high-rise buildings. It is now difficult for the wealthy to flee from busy urban areas to places of quiet seclusion, because so many more people can afford to go with them. *The elite's environmental deterioration is often the common man's improved standard of living.*

Our soaring aspirations

A somewhat different factor which has contributed to greater concern with environmental quality is a marked increase in our aspirations and standards concerning what our environment ought to be like. In my opinion, rising dissatisfaction with the "system" in the United States does not result primarily from poorer performance by that system. Rather, it stems mainly from a rapid escalation of our aspirations as to what the system's performance ought to be. Nowhere is this phenomenon more striking than in regard to the quality of the environment. One hundred years ago, white Americans were eliminating whole Indian tribes without a qualm. Today, many serious-minded citizens seek to make important issues out of the potential disappearance of the whooping crane, the timber wolf, and other exotic creatures. Meanwhile, thousands of Indians in Brazil are still being murdered each year—but American conservationists are not focusing on that human massacre. Similarly, some aesthetes decry "galloping sprawl" in metropolitan fringe areas, while they ignore acres of rat-infested housing a few miles away. Hence the escalation of our environmental aspirations is more selective than might at first appear.

Yet regarding many forms of pollution, we are now rightly upset over practices and conditions that have largely been ignored for decades. An example is our alarm about the dumping of industrial wastes and sewage into rivers and lakes. This increase in our environmental aspirations is part of a general cultural phenomenon stimulated both by our success in raising living standards and by the recent emphases of the communications media. Another cause of the rapid rise in interest in environmental pollution is the "explosion" of alarmist rhetoric on this subject. According to some well-publicized experts, all life on earth is threatened by an "environmental crisis." Some claim human life will end within three decades or less if we do not do something drastic about current behavior patterns.

Are things really that bad? Frankly, I am not enough of an ecological expert to know. But I am skeptical concerning all highly alarmist views because so many previous prophets of doom and disaster have been so wrong concerning many other so-called "crises" in our society.

There are two reasonable definitions of "crisis." One kind of crisis consists of a rapidly deteriorating situation moving towards a single disastrous event at some future moment. The second kind consists of a more gradually deteriorating situation that will eventually pass some subtle "point of no return." At present, I do not believe either of these definitions applies to most American domestic problems. Although many social critics hate to admit it, the American "system" actually serves the majority of citizens rather well in terms of most indicators of well-being. Concerning such things as real income, personal mobility, variety and choice of consumption patterns, longevity, health, leisure time, and quality of housing, most Americans are better off today than they have ever been and extraordinarily better off than most of mankind. What is *not* improving is the gap between society's performance and what most people—or at least highly vocal minorities—believe society *ought* to be doing to solve these problems. Our aspirations and standards have risen far faster than the beneficial outputs of our social system. Therefore, although most Americans, including most of the poor, are receiving more now, they are enjoying it less.

This conclusion should not be confused with the complacency of some super-patriots. It would be unrealistic to deny certain important negative trends in American life. Some conditions are indeed getting worse for nearly everyone. Examples are air quality and freedom from thievery. Moreover, congestion and environmental deterioration might forever destroy certain valuable national amenities if they are not checked. Finally, there has probably been a general rise in personal and social anxiety in recent years. I believe this is due to increased tensions caused by our rapid rate of technical and social change, plus the increase in worldwide communication through the media. These developments rightly cause serious and genuine concern among millions of Americans.

The future of the environmental issue

Concern about the environment has passed through the first two stages of the "issue-attention cycle" and is by now well into the third. In fact, we have already begun to move toward the fourth stage, in which the intensity of public interest in environmental improvement must inexorably decline. And this raises an interesting question: Will the issue of environmental quality then move on into the "post-problem" stage of the cycle?

My answer to this question is: Yes, but not soon, because certain characteristics of this issue will protect it from the rapid decline in public interest typical of many other recent issues. First of all, many kinds of environmental pollution are much more visible and more clearly threatening than most other social problems. This is particularly true of air pollution. The greater the apparent threat from visible forms of pollution and the more vividly this can be dramatized, the more public support environmental improvement will receive and the longer it will sustain public interest. Ironically, the cause of ecologists would therefore benefit from an environmental disaster like a "killer smog" that would choke thousands to death in a few days. Actually, this is nothing new; every cause from early Christianity to the Black Panthers has benefited from martyrs. Yet even the most powerful symbols lose their impact if they are constantly repeated. The piteous sight of an oil-soaked seagull or a dead soldier pales after it has been viewed even a dozen times. Moreover, some of the worst environmental threats come from forms of pollution that are invisible. Thus, our propensity to focus attention on what is most visible may cause us to clean up the pollution we can easily perceive while ignoring even more dangerous but hidden threats.

Pollution is also likely to be kept in the public eye because it is an issue that threatens almost everyone, not just a small percentage of the population. Since it is not politically divisive, politicians can safely pursue it without fearing adverse repercussions. Attacking environmental pollution is therefore much safer than attacking racism or poverty. For an attack upon the latter antagonizes important blocs of voters who benefit from the sufferings of others or at least are not threatened enough by such suffering to favor spending substantial amounts of their money to reduce it.

A third strength of the environmental issue is that much of the "blame" for pollution can be attributed to a small group of "villains" whose wealth and power make them excellent scapegoats. Environmental defenders can therefore "courageously" attack these scapegoats without antagonizing most citizens. Moreover, at least in regard to air pollution, that small group actually has enough power greatly to reduce pollution if it really tries. If leaders of the nation's top auto-producing, power-generating, and fuel-supplying firms would change their behavior significantly, a drastic decline in air pollution could be achieved very quickly. This has been demonstrated at many locations already.

Gathering support for attacking any problem is always easier if its ills can be blamed on a small number of "public enemies"—as is shown by the success of Ralph Nader. This tactic is especially effective if the "enemies" exhibit extreme wealth and power, eccentric dress and manners, obscene language, or some other uncommon traits. Then society can aim its outrage at a small, alien group without having to face up to the need to alter its own behavior. It is easier to find such scapegoats for almost all forms of pollution than for other major problems like poverty, poor housing, or racism. Solutions to those problems would require millions of Americans to change their own behavior patterns, to accept higher taxes, or both.

The possibility that technological solutions can be devised for most

pollution problems may also lengthen the public prominence of this
issue. To the extent that pollution can be reduced through technological change, most people's basic attitudes, expectations, and behavior patterns will not have to be altered. The traumatic difficulties
of achieving major institutional change could thus be escaped through
the "magic" of purely technical improvements in automobile engines,
water purification devices, fuel composition, and sewage treatment
facilities.

Financing the fight against pollution

Another aspect of anti-pollution efforts that will strengthen their
political support is that most of the costs can be passed on to the
public through higher product prices rather than higher taxes. Therefore, politicians can demand enforcement of costly environmental
quality standards without paying the high political price of raising
the required funds through taxes. True, water pollution is caused
mainly by the actions of public bodies, especially municipal sewer
systems, and effective remedies for this form of pollution require
higher taxes or at least higher prices for public services. But the major
costs of reducing most kinds of pollution can be added to product
prices and thereby quietly shifted to the ultimate consumers of the
outputs concerned. This is a politically painless way to pay for attacking a major social problem. In contrast, effectively combatting most
social problems requires large-scale income redistribution attainable
only through both higher taxes and higher transfer payments or subsidies. Examples of such politically costly problems are poverty, slum
housing, low-quality health care for the poor, and inadequate public
transportation.

Many ecologists oppose paying for a cleaner environment through
higher product prices. They would rather force the polluting firms to
bear the required costs through lower profits. In a few oligopolistic
industries, like petroleum and automobile production, this might
work. But in the long run, not much of the total cost could be paid
this way without driving capital out of the industries concerned and
thereby eventually forcing product prices upwards. Furthermore, it is
just that those who use any given product should pay the full cost of
making it—including the cost of avoiding excessive pollution in its
production. Such payment is best made through higher product
prices. In my opinion, it would be unwise in most cases to try to pay
these costs by means of government subsidies in order to avoid shifting the load onto consumers. We need to conserve our politically

limited taxing capabilities to attack those problems that cannot be dealt with in any other way.

Still another reason why the cleaner-environment issue may last a long time is that it could generate a large private industry with strong vested interests in continued spending against pollution. Already dozens of firms with "eco-" or "environ-" in their names have sprung up to exploit supposedly burgeoning anti-pollution markets. In time, we might even generate an "environmental-industrial complex" about which some future President could vainly warn us in his retirement speech! Any issue gains longevity if its sources of political support and the programs related to it can be institutionalized in large bureaucracies. Such organizations have a powerful desire to keep public attention focused on the problems that support them. However, it is doubtful that the anti-pollution industry will ever come close to the defense industry in size and power. Effective anti-pollution activities cannot be carried out separately from society as a whole because they require changes in behavior by millions of people. In contrast, weapons are produced by an industry that imposes no behavioral changes (other than higher taxes) on the average citizen.

Finally, environmental issues may remain at center stage longer than most domestic issues because of their very ambiguity. "Improving the environment" is a tremendously broad and all-encompassing objective. Almost everyone can plausibly claim that his or her particular cause is another way to upgrade the quality of our life. This ambiguity will make it easier to form a majority-sized coalition favoring a variety of social changes associated with improving the environment. The inability to form such a coalition regarding problems that adversely affect only minority-sized groups usually hastens the exit of such problems from the center of public attention.

All the factors set forth above indicate that circumstances are unusually favorable for launching and sustaining major efforts to improve the quality of our environment. Yet we should not underestimate the American public's capacity to become bored—especially with something that does not immediately threaten them, or promise huge benefits for a majority, or strongly appeal to their sense of injustice. In the present mood of the nation, I believe most citizens do not want to confront the need for major social changes on any issues except those that seem directly to threaten them—such as crime and other urban violence. And even in regard to crime, the public does not yet wish to support really effective changes in our basic system of justice. The present Administration has apparently concluded that a relatively "low-profile" government—one that does not try to lead the public into accepting truly significant institutional changes—will most please the majority of Americans at this point. Regardless of the accuracy of this view, if it remains dominant within the federal government, then no major environmental programs are likely to receive long-sustained public attention or support.

Some proponents of improving the environment are relying on the support of students and other young people to keep this issue at the center of public attention. Such support, however, is not adequate as a long-term foundation. Young people form a highly unstable base for the support of any policy because they have such short-lived "staying power." For one thing, they do not long enjoy the large amount of free time they possess while in college. Also, as new individuals enter the category of "young people" and older ones leave it, different issues are stressed and accumulated skills in marshaling opinion are dissipated. Moreover, the radicalism of the young has been immensely exaggerated by the media's tendency to focus attention upon those with extremist views. In their attitudes toward political issues, most young people are not very different from their parents.

There is good reason, then, to believe that the bundle of issues called "improving the environment" will also suffer the gradual loss of public attention characteristic of the later stages of the "issue-attention cycle." However, it will be eclipsed at a much slower rate than other recent domestic issues. So it may be possible to accomplish some significant improvements in environmental quality—if those seeking them work fast.

12

Separating the Planning and Procurement of Public Services from Their Production and Delivery

1972-73

The fastest growing part of the American economy since 1950 has been the public sector, especially state and local governments. Employment by all governments now exceeds 18 percent of all civilian nonagricultural employment—the highest level in American history. Even more striking, from 1950 through 1970, around 33 percent of all *net additions* to total civilian employment consisted of new government jobs. From 1970 to October 1974, state and local government employment rose by 1,775,000—22.5 percent of the total national gain in civilian employment, and 26 percent of that in civilian nonagricultural employment.

These facts emphasize the vital importance of improving human resource productivity in the public sector as a means of increasing the economy's total output. Yet productivity gains in the public sector have historically lagged far behind those in the private sector. At least that appears to be the case, based upon the highly imperfect available measures of human resource productivity in both sectors. This article examines some major deficiencies in the current use of human resources in the public sector. It then proposes a new approach to remedying those deficiencies by altering the institutional structure of many

Revised version of a speech presented to a Conference on Problems of Growth and Development in the Great Lakes Region (Chicago, October 18, 1972) and to the Annual Meeting of the Council of State Planning Agencies (San Francisco, February 15, 1973).

agencies now responsible for producing public services. Public education in big cities is used as an example of how this approach might be applied.

THREE MAJOR DEFICIENCIES IN PRESENT PUBLIC SECTOR USE OF HUMAN RESOURCES

Inadequate Incentives for Improving Individual Productivity

The public sector provides extremely ineffective incentives for either workers or managers to improve the amount of useful output per unit of input. The most striking examples of this deficiency is the constant pressure from public employees for higher wages without any offsetting increases in productivity, or at least none that are visible. Local citizens are paying teachers, policemen, firemen, and other "public servants" more and more money to do no more work—and in some cases, to do less work. This is an economically untenable situation in the long run. After all, society cannot increase the *total per-member compensation* of all its members unless their *total per-member productivity rises.* This is obvious when we consider society as a whole. But whenever any one group in society gets higher pay with no higher productivity, the members of that group are redistributing incomes to themselves at the expense of others. In the last decade, municipal employees have been redistributing incomes to themselves from other municipal taxpayers. Because of the regressive nature of most city tax structures, this means middle-class teachers and other city workers have been enriching themselves at the expense of the urban poor, without providing much added service to the poor in return.

Admittedly, it is very difficult to measure productivity in most public sector jobs. Their outputs are partly intangible, and we have failed to define those outputs very carefully. Therefore, public workers may have been improving their productivity somewhat in hard-to-measure ways. Nevertheless, it seems clear to me that we have greatly increased salary payments to educators in recent years without a commensurate rise in output.

For example, per-pupil spending in Chicago's public schools rose 48 percent from 1967 to 1971, and the vast majority of that increase consisted of higher teachers' salaries. During those four years, the consumer price index rose 21 percent. Judging from parental complaints about the schools, it is questionable whether per-pupil educational outputs rose at all. They certainly did not increase 48 percent, or even 20 percent. So Chicago and other Illinois taxpayers are paying a lot more per pupil and getting very little more—if anything—in return.

The blame for this undesirable outcome rests with public sector *managers* as well as public sector employees. The prevailing incentives for government managers do not reward more effective use of human resources as much as they reward certain other activities. These include building staff empires, pleasing constituents who want expanded services, and avoiding political controversy. Hence, managerial incentives aggravate the cost-expanding tendency of employee incentives, instead of counteracting them as in the private sector.

Why are public sector incentives for efficiency so weak? I believe the main reason is the relative *monopoly of supply* enjoyed by producers of most public services. Unlike the consumers of private goods that are available from any of several competitive suppliers, the consumers of federal, state, and local government services cannot easily influence their suppliers by threatening to take their patronage elsewhere. True, consumers of public services provided by any government can theoretically express dissatisfaction by moving into the territory of some other government. Yet such inter-governmental competition provides almost no check on the monopolistic position of the federal government, not much check on that of state governments, and only a limited check on that of even local governments. For one thing, moving is difficult and expensive; so public services must become highly undesirable before a household shifts its location just to improve them. Moreover, most households are geographically linked to employment in some way; hence, they can choose only among those localities within commuting range of the jobs involved. Even more important, many low-income households living in older central-city neighborhoods cannot afford any of the housing and private transportation in surrounding suburbs. Consequently, the poor are a "captive market" for the agencies providing public services in the central cities concerned.

Producer Dominance in Determining What Services Are Provided

A second major deficiency in the present provision of most public services is that the producers themselves largely determine what consumers will receive. Neither the consumers nor those who pay for such services—taxpayers in general—have much to say about what is to be produced or how it is to be delivered. The producers defend this arrangement by claiming the services involved are too technically complex for "mere laymen" to understand. But thousands of commercially produced products, such as television sets, computers, and automobiles, are equally complex, yet consumers exercise a great deal of influence upon what they receive by choosing from among many different products offered by competing suppliers.

In competitive markets, consumers "vote with their dollars," thereby raising total demand for products they like and lowering it for those they dislike. Producers rapidly respond by increasing the output of much-demanded items (such as small cars) and reducing that of little-demanded items (such as the Edsel). Thus, the technical complexity of products need not eliminate consumer influence over output, as long as there is significant competition among sources of supply. It is the *monopoly of supply sources* that deprives consumers and tax-payers of meaningful participation in determining output.

Unfortunately, whenever the *members* of any production organization become more influential in determining what it produces than its consumers, those members invariably shape their decisions primarily to promote their own survival and convenience. They make decisions about what is produced, how much it costs, and how it is delivered so as to serve their own interests first and the interests of consumers last. Of course, this producer-serving bias is obscured by a fog of public relations rhetoric that claims just the opposite.

Yet one of the major conclusions in my book, *Inside Bureaucracy*,[1] is that large bureaucracies almost *never* carry out major changes in their behavior as a result of purely internal developments, including internal decisions that services ought to be improved. Rather, major changes nearly always occur because of intensive pressure from outside the organizations themselves. That pressure can take any one of three basic forms: *increased competition* (other sources of supply who say they can do it better); *starvation* (major slashes in budgets that require big changes in behavior); or *flooding with new resources and new demands* (as NASA was flooded when the U.S. decided to put men on the moon). In my opinion, applying these external pressures is the only way to make providers of public services more responsive to consumer needs and desires than they are now.

Where these external pressures are lacking, provision of public services becomes dominated by rules and decisions that sacrifice the interests of consumers to the benefit of producers. For example, in big-city public schools, increased funds are used far more for higher administrator and teacher salaries than for broadened services, improved equipment and books, or more parent counseling. Teachers unions impose one rule that allows the most experienced teachers to choose where they will be located and another rule prohibiting payment of differential salaries for locating them in the lowest-income schools where they are most needed. Both unions and administrators oppose even experimenting with widespread use of performance measurement or merit pay to give the highest rewards to the most effective teachers. I realize there are plausible arguments in favor of these

---

[1] Anthony Downs, *Inside Bureaucracy* (Boston: Little, Brown, 1967), pp. 191–210.

decisions. Yet the net impression one gets from studying big-city bureaucracies is that most of their administrative decisions and arrangements are designed to benefit their own members, often at the expense of improved consumer convenience or higher output.

Lack of a Powerful Consumer-Oriented Intermediary in the Service Production Process

In theory, elected politicians represent the citizenry in general in dealing with agencies that supply public services. Governors, mayors, legislators, and other elected officials are supposed to influence public bureaucracies so the latter provide what the citizens want. But this "consumer advocacy" role of elected officials has been tremendously weakened. As a result of the three factors discussed below, no powerful, persistent consumer-oriented force strongly influences the production of most public services.

The first weakening factor is the "removal from politics" of certain service-producing bureaucracies that have succeeded in "professionalizing" themselves. Examples are most school systems and many police departments. This shift from former political control of service production to civil service or professionalism occurred in response to past corruption and undesirable patronage practices. Hence, this change achieved certain very desirable results. But the price has been to render these agencies far less responsive to consumer demands than they would be if they were more politically sensitive. In fact, in many areas, rigid civil service rules make it almost impossible even to discharge grossly incompetent workers, let alone change well-entrenched policies. I believe the pendulum of change has now swung too far away from political sensitivity.

The "consumer advocacy" role of many elected officials is also weakened by their identification as *heads of service production* in their own minds and in those of the public. Governors and mayors in particular are considered the chief administrators of public agencies providing many services. As such, they are held responsible for what those agencies do. Consequently, they often adopt a defensive stance towards agency behavior rather than an aggressive "consumer ombudsman" stance. This weakens both their ability and their willingness to impose consumer desires on those agencies whenever doing so either reduces the convenience of agency members or implies that present agency actions are ineffective.

The third factor weakening the "consumer-advocacy" of elected officials is their lack of capabilities for evaluating the outputs of public service agencies. Few governors, mayors, or legislators have large enough personal staffs to effectively analyze the activities of the many huge bureaucracies theoretically under their jurisdiction. In order to conduct such analyses, they must rely heavily upon data and even studies produced by members of the agencies being evaluated. This procedure does not lead to the most objective or penetrating results, for obvious reasons. Moreover, most elected officials are strongly oriented towards relatively short-run concerns keyed to the date of the next election. Hence, they tend to allocate their limited analytic re-sources to "fighting fires" caused by immediate "crises" rather than to conducting longer range studies of agency performance or con-sumer desires. Furthermore, chief executives must expend much of their energy trying to achieve a workable balance of resources among many different agencies rather than becoming familiar in detail with the workings or inadequacies of any of them.

As a result of these three factors, the effectiveness of most elected officials in acting as "consumer advocates" against public service agencies has been seriously reduced. This is one reason why so many "consumer advocate" groups are dissatisfied with the claims of state and local government officials that the present processes of repre-sentative government adequately protect consumer interests. Such ineffectiveness is also a cause of the recent demand for more direct "citizen participation" in public decisions, such as the location of new highways and the construction of power generation facilities. Yet no really satisfactory institutions have yet been devised for achieving effective consumer representation in the process of producing most public services. What we need is a powerful consumer-oriented actor who is much closer to the service-production process than the chief executive can possibly be. In fact, this probably requires a strong con-sumer advocate concerning each major type of public service, whose role is strategically structured in the midst of the process of producing that service.

SOME CRITERIA FOR INSTITUTIONAL STRUCTURES THAT WOULD IMPROVE FUTURE USE OF HUMAN RESOURCES IN THE PUBLIC SECTOR

Clearly, it would be desirable to devise institutional structures that would help remedy the above-described deficiencies in public-sector use of human resources. The first step toward doing so is to formulate some specific characteristics—or criteria of desirability—that any such structure should possess. Four such criteria derived from the above analysis are as follows:

1. *Each such institutional arrangement should emphasize defining specific service outputs, measuring the effectiveness of producers in creating those outputs, and making the results known to consumers.*

Although participants in, and observers of, the public sector have been talking about doing this for a long time, not much real progress has been made. The main reason is that only the service-producing agencies themselves possess the resources and information required to define and measure outputs. Yet they have strong incentives not to do so, because no organization—or person—likes being objectively evaluated. Those agencies or other parties with strong incentives to perform such evaluations have not had the information or resources required. We need to combine both the capabilities and the incentives in a single organization that is closely related to the service production process.

2. *Each such institutional arrangement should shift more choices about what services will be produced and how they will be delivered directly to consumers themselves.* Consumers can then play a stronger role in setting goals and allocating resources through their choices. But consumers can exercise meaningful choices only if they can select among differing services or means of delivery offered by alternative sources of supply. So *creating greater consumer choice requires creating competition of some type 'within each presently monolithic supply source, or among different sources of supply,* perhaps including private sources. There is no other way.

3. *The compensation of the managers and employees in each such institution should be closely linked to their performances in producing the desired outputs.* This means that salaries and incentive payments would be significantly tied to production and efficiency, not primarily to longevity, educational qualifications, seniority, union bargaining power, or other strictly input characteristics. Conforming to this criterion may require adopting some compensation schemes that seem almost revolutionary for the public sector. Admittedly, this will not be easy to achieve in the face of bitter opposition from the service-producing agencies themselves. Nevertheless, I believe we must begin confronting the need to create public sector institutions that provide effective incentives for improved performance rather than mainly rewarding mere survival or avoidance of controversy.

4. *Each such institutional structure should act as a consumer-oriented counterforce to producer domination of the public service production and delivery process.* To do this, the new structure must be located very close to the production process for the specific service or type of service concerned and must be fully informed about what goes on in that process. Yet it must not be responsible for service production or delivery.

Undoubtedly, additional criteria of desirability for such institutions could be formulated. But these four—all derived from the preceding analysis—already pose a difficult enough challenge for the remainder of this article.

SEPARATING THE PLANNING AND PROCUREMENT OF PUBLIC SERVICES FROM THEIR PRODUCTION AND DELIVERY

At first glance, it may seem impossible to design any institutional structure capable of meeting the above criteria. However, the Citizens League of the Twin Cities Area has suggested an approach that I believe has an excellent chance of working quite well. This approach is described at length in their outstanding report, *Why Not Buy Public Services?* I have borrowed many ideas from that report, and the remainder of this paper represents my expanded and somewhat modified version of the basic concept suggested by the Citizens League.

The essence of this concept is separating the *planning* and *procurement* of public services from their *production* and *delivery*. This could be done institutionally by altering the functions of the present leadership in each major public service agency from *producing outputs* to *procuring services produced by others*. The leadership would have to stop thinking of itself as in charge of creating services and start thinking of itself as solely a procurement agent serving consumers.

A striking example of such an orientation in modern bureaucracies is provided by Robert McNamara. When he became Secretary of Defense, he deliberately separated himself from the three armed services, who are the *producers* of national defense. He rapidly built up his own staff of analytic experts entirely different in character, abilities, and background from the staffs of the armed services. He created this large "counterstaff" so he could develop his own studies and recommendations independently from those provided to him by the producer-dominated staffs of the armed services. In essence, he viewed himself as a procurer of defense services, not a producer thereof. Although some of his major decisions later proved mistaken, I believe his basic conception of the secretary's role was sound. Unfortunately, the defense bureaucracy is so large that trying to control it in this manner tends to exemplify one of Downs's Laws of Bureaucracy: Any attempt to control one large bureaucracy begets another. Nevertheless, creation of a sizable "counterstaff" in the office of the chief executive (who should really be seen as the chief *service purchaser*) is probably a necessary price for meeting the criteria set forth above.

In the case of local or state government, we could divorce the present head of each major service-production agency from responsibility for service production, and instead conceive of him or her as responsible for the planning and procurement of certain services desired by the public. At first, the vast majority of those services would probably be procured directly from the public agency that now produces them. But separating planning and procurement from production and delivery would immediately produce some favorable results. For one thing, since the agency head would no longer be responsible for service production, he or she would be far more willing to try objectively to define desired outputs and measure the effectiveness of the production agency in creating them. Second, this official would no longer have a vested interest in maintaining the present organizational arrangement of the service-production agency. Hence, the official would be more willing to act as an *external force* pressuring that agency to change so as to serve consumer needs and desires more effectively, even when doing so required changes inconvenient or threatening to the existing production bureaucracy. If we defined the official's role in terms of maintaining such an advocacy posture, we could expect a marked shift in the behavior of agency heads.

However, in the long run, these officials could put really effective pressure on service-production agencies to change only if they had the ability to select alternative sources of supply. Presumably, they would do so only when the agencies failed to produce what the officials thought would best serve consumers. But how can true competition be created for a large monopolistic service-production agency like a local school system?

I do not believe this can be done immediately concerning all aspects of the services produced by such an agency, except through radical and disruptive institutional changes that are not very likely to be adopted. However, a significant *marginal* increase in competition could be created without unduly disrupting existing institutions if the scope and variety of the services to be procured by a single "consumer advocate" were broadened so that more than one *existing* production agency was involved. These agencies would all produce services that are seen as essentially different *from the producers' viewpoint* but are seen as closely related or overlapping *from the consumers' viewpoint.* If several such agencies were placed under a single *consumer service procurement agent,* that agent could put pressure on each agency to change by proposing to shift a marginal amount of its existing resources to one of the other agencies that served some relevant consumer need better. This process is often used within the Defense Department concerning activities that serve the same *output function* (for example, destroying enemy targets with nuclear weapons) but use very different *processes of production* (for example, jet bombers vs. submarine-based ballistic missiles).

Such marginal-change pressure can be created only when different service-production agencies produce outputs that perform somewhat overlapping or closely related functions in the lives of their users. Yet this is a far more common occurrence than most people realize, particularly when both *private* and *public* service producers are taken into account simultaneously. Moreover, "threats" of marginal reallocations among already existing agencies could create immediate competitive pressure on all those concerned *without* requiring generation of whole new production agencies. This is far *less* threatening to existing bureaucracies—and less costly—than trying to create a whole new organization to compete across-the-board with each existing agency.

A public service planning and procurement agency could also pressure public service-production agencies to change their behavior by developing alternative sources of supplies within the private sector. True, where any large, presently monopolistic public bureau is concerned, it would be impossible to seek private suppliers for all or even most of the services provided by that bureau, at least not in any relatively short time period. The public school system in a large city could not feasibly be suddenly displaced by one or even many private suppliers of education. Nevertheless, a separate planning and procurement agency could effectively influence at least some of the public school system's behavior by proposing to move marginal amounts of its activities into the private sector. The mere solicitation of proposals for such a shift from private producers might stimulate considerable innovation or at least flexibility within that part of the public agency likely to be cut back. Furthermore, if even small amounts of the public bureau's existing activities were successfully transferred to private suppliers, that would act as a demonstration of what might be done elsewhere in the bureau. Thus, it could have a far-reaching impact upon the entire bureau, causing much more sensitivity to both costs and consumer desires than now exists.

In my opinion, creation of at least the *possibility* of procuring some presently publicly supplied services from the private sector is a key reason for separating the planning and procurement of public services from their production and delivery, as proposed above. In fact, this has already been accomplished concerning higher education in some states. In Illinois, for example, a single Board of Higher Education is responsible for planning major educational strategy for all publicly financed institutions of higher education, but not for administering any production of educational services. Since public scholarship funds can be used in either private or public colleges and universities, the board must take both into account in looking at future educational needs in the state. This arrangement not only separates some of the planning of public services from their production, but also gives consumers themselves a major role in deciding how public funds will be allocated among competing producers in both the public and private sectors.

AN EXAMPLE: PUBLIC EDUCATION IN LARGE CITIES

Some Major Deficiencies in Present Big-City Schools

To illustrate the above-described approach, let us examine how it might be applied to public secondary school education in large cities. I have chosen this example partly because provision of this service is widely considered to be inadequate, ineffective, and unresponsive to true consumer needs and desires. However, I wish to emphasize that my comments are preliminary, tentative, and incomplete. They are meant to suggest an approach that requires a great deal more thought and exploration before it can be put into practice.

In many big cities, our most inadequate public schools are part of our general failure to cope with urban poverty. I conceive of poverty in America as primarily a *relative* phenomenon, following the theories of Lee Rainwater. Poverty-related behavior patterns arise because people feel *left out* of society. They are unable to participate in what Rainwater calls *validating activities*—uses of their time that are re-garded as meaningful and rewarding by themselves and others. One of the most important types of validating activities is employment in a steady and rewarding job.

Our big cities now fail to provide many young people with work opportunities that are linked closely enough to public schools to make what happens in those schools seem significant to the students. For example, the schools are not successful in teaching many young peo-ple such vital basic work disciplines as daily attendance, reasonable punctuality, and willingness to follow simple instructions. Presumably, one reason why young people are not interested in absorbing these disciplines from their education is that there seems to be no relation-ship between what happens in school and access to good jobs.

Jobs are controlled for the most part by private firms and schools are controlled by a public bureaucracy. No one agent or actor with control or even influence over both has the function of trying to end unemployment among young people by closely tying their schooling to job opportunities. Presumably, if students were convinced that learn-ing well what was taught in school would *guarantee* them a job, and failing to learn would prevent their employment, they would be far more strongly motivated to apply themselves in school. But that im-plies a much closer and stronger link between schools and jobs than now exists. It would require very significant changes in the behavior of both private employers and public schools and perhaps extension of the recent public jobs program. Yet lack of constructive employment opportunities for young people is probably a major cause of such key urban ills as high crime rates, drug addiction, broken families, and juvenile delinquency. Consequently, effective remedial action is certainly worth pursuing.

Creating a "Board of Maturation"

Why not seek to remedy this situation by having state and local governments view secondary education, vocational education, job training, job creation, and even youth employment as diverse parts of a single process—the maturation of young people? If this perspective prevailed, then the planning and procurement of *all* these "outputs" could be viewed as the responsibility of a single overseeing "consumer advocate" agency within each community. That agency would be in charge of helping consumers procure services from the many different organizations—both public and private—that now produce these varied services. The new "consumer advocate" agency might be called —at least for reference in this article—the "Board of Maturation" or the "Youth Development Board" instead of the "Board of Education." The basic responsibility of this board would be to insure that every young person in the community received assistance in developing adequate skills for assuming a productive adult role in society. Rather than channeling all young people along the same path to maturity (such as formal education), it would seek to create a variety of different possible paths and to counsel each family so that its offspring followed the paths best suited for them individually.

The board would receive all the public funds now directed at these different agencies. It would be responsible for allocating those funds in the manner that procured the best "bundle" of services for each of the consumers it was serving. This might require it to alter present allocations among the several service-production agencies concerned. The board would also have to develop much more explicit relationships between educational institutions and private firms that employ young workers. In this case, it would not control the funding underlying those jobs, since that would be part of the internal economics of the firms concerned. Nevertheless, it might be able to supplement private wages with public training or employment funds in ways that would give private employers strong incentives to cooperate closely with the board.

This reorganization of what is now the Board of Education in most communities would require significant restructuring of the existing public bureaucracy. When transformed into the Board of Maturation, this organization would cease to be responsible for *producing* education. Instead, it would become a consumer-oriented agency responsible for helping consumers plan what youth development services they needed and then helping them procure those services from a variety of sources. Undoubtedly, most of the planning and procurement would at first be done by the board and its staff rather than by consumers themselves. But greater consumer participation could evolve in the future, especially if the board set up a counseling service as one of its major functions.

The separation of this board from the existing public school system would require designating the present administrators of the school system as responsible for its *production* activities. Thus, the Superintendent of Schools would become the head of the school system seen as a service production and delivery system. Since he was formerly the head of the staff for the board, the board would need a new professional staff to advise it and carry out the day-to-day functions of service planning and procurement. Hence, this separation of functions appears to multiply the number of levels in the bureaucracy, making red tape worse instead of better.

But this apparent deterioration would be more than offset by an added element of interbureau competition. Such competition would be created by broadening the board's scope to include the activities of other service-production agencies besides the public school system. Then, as noted above, the board could make—or "threaten" to make— at least marginal shifts of resources among these agencies where their services overlapped in terms of their function for consumers. The increased competition among these agencies in these overlapping areas would force them to become more innovative, flexible, and sensitive to consumer desires than they are now. Hopefully, these effects would produce significant net benefits in spite of the added layer of bureaucracy represented by the board's own staff. In fact, I believe this basic change in structure might produce a whole new public service environment. If it worked, it would introduce powerful consumer advocacy into the heart of the service production processes now almost totally dominated by producers themselves.

This new structure is compatible with several different kinds of funding arrangements. It could be based upon pooling the funds now used by the public agencies concerned, while raising funds the same way they are raised now. Or it could be linked to new funding ideas, such as the "educational trust fund" concept proposed by Edward Clarke and John Fyfe in a recent paper.[2] They suggested that each

---

[2] Edward H. Clarke, "The Education and Training Investment Program," and John Fyfe, "The Effectiveness of Education: Some Guides to Education Finance Reform," in Selma Mushkin, Ed., *State Aids for Human Services in a Federal System* (Washington, D.C.: Public Services Laboratory of Georgetown University, May 1974).

state guarantee all students a basic minimum level of public school funding (a "first tier"). It would also provide a "second tier" in the form of a per-student allowance controlled by the parents, which could be used for conventional schooling, vocational schooling, other job training, or even a wage subsidy. This would provide a strong element of consumer choice in determining how public funds were to be used in providing the optimal maturation path for each child. Still other forms of funding could be adapted to the basic approach suggested in this paper.

Whatever funding mechanism was used, I believe it should provide consumers with a significant element of choice in determining how the public funds assigned to their children should be used to help those children reach maturity. This would require a major new input of consumer counseling services. It might involve development of several alternative "packages" of maturation-aiding programs tailored to different types of young people. Students in public high schools already exercise significant degrees of choice among subjects—and even among schools. Hence, it would not be beyond their capabilities— assisted by their parents and some added counseling—to exercise similar choices among different combinations and sequences of conventional schooling, vocational education, on-the-job training, and part-time or full-time employment.

A BRIEF LOOK AT A SECOND EXAMPLE

The idea of combining (1) separation of service planning and procurement from production and delivery and (2) a broadened scope of services under the purview of a single "consumer advocate" agency could also be applied to many other types of public services. I have not tried to run down the standard list of government services to see how well it fits each of those normally provided, though I believe this should be done. But I can suggest one other potentially fruitful possibility. At present, most local police departments both enforce the law and provide a variety of social services unrelated to law enforcement but derived from their 24-hour availability and immediate responsiveness to calls for help. Why not redesignate the police commissioner as the Commissioner of Law Enforcement and On-Site Social Services? This might shift his perspective significantly, especially if his purview were broadened to incorporate some private security agencies and some social welfare and emergency aid organizations. Rather than attempting to explore all the ramifications of this suggestion, I will provocatively leave them for readers to ponder.

SOME UNRESOLVED DIFFICULTIES

Admittedly, the basic approach proposed in this article involves many potential problems and difficulties that I have not confronted. These include the following:

1. How could a Board of Maturation enlist the close cooperation of business firms needed to more fully integrate work experiences and work opportunities with public education?
2. How could society keep the Board of Maturation—or any comparable agency—from drifting away from a consumer-advocacy posture towards a producer-advocacy posture as most regulatory agencies originally set up to "police" specific industries have done in the past? (Examples are the Interstate Commerce Commission, the Federal Power Commission, and the Federal Communications Commission.)
3. What specific funding arrangements would be used to finance the added activities required by the board's new staff?
4. How would this entire institutional structure be related to property taxation in a manner that would satisfy the new legal challenges to traditional educational funding?

I do not pretend to have answered these questions or even to have raised all the key challenges to this approach that could be made. Nor can I do so within the confines of this article. Nevertheless, I believe the application of this approach to the field of education does offer hope of achieving something many observers have long believed crucial: a broadening of the number of respectable paths to maturity that society makes available and attractive to young people. We need this so the many young people not suited to the presently dominant college-degree path can find alternatives that are equally satisfying psychologically, financially, and in terms of both their self-respect and the respect of society generally. The fact that this general approach at least in theory offers a means of attaining this key goal makes me believe it is well worth analyzing further.

CONCLUSION

The major purpose of this paper has been to stimulate further exploration of this whole approach rather than to urge its immediate application. Our need to improve the way we use human resources in the public sector is already urgent. It will become even more crucial as

242   Urban Problems and Prospects

government employment becomes a larger percentage of our total labor force and government decisions assume greater importance in shaping our entire society. I believe there is enough promise of major improvement in the concept of separating the planning and procurement of public services from their production and delivery to warrant intensive and widespread evaluation of this idea at all levels of government, especially the state and local levels. If we can introduce a powerful consumer advocate into the heart of the service-production process, generate some innovation-stimulating competition among public agencies, and help consumers greatly expand their own choices, we may work a quiet but immensely important revolution in the public sector.

[8]

They sell sizzle, but their predictions fizzle

As a writer of many carefully researched studies with sales resembling soccer-team scores, I view the fantastic publishing success of what I call 'exagger-books' with mixed emotions. On the one hand, I admire the new ideas and insights that authors like Alvin Toffler, John Naisbitt, and Marilyn Ferguson present in their bestselling works. Moreover, I frankly envy their enormous sales and instant fame. On the other hand, I deplore the falsity of both methods and conclusions typical of such books.

True, all authors overemphasize their main themes somewhat. But exagger-book writers wildly inflate whatever trends, evils, or other phenomena they have discovered. To 'prove' their vastly over-blown hypotheses, they pile up tons of often irrelevant but plausible sounding anecdotes masquerading as facts. I call it 'mega-hyping the pseudo-facts'.

Exagger-books are neither new nor confined to studies of the future. Vance Packard sold millions of them in the '50s and '60s by 'exposing' evil tendencies he claimed were about to engulf society. More recently, various self-proclaimed gurus like Howard Ruff made fortunes by promising salvation from imminent but not-yet-here collapses in stocks, real estate, world banking and the economy generally.

But recent exagger-authors have raised the art of pseudo-scientific hyperbole to new heights. Shrewdly, they focus mainly on long-range forces, so it takes many years for events to contradict their forecasts. And since they are intuitively projecting 'trends' they have perceived in recent events, they cannot be held to rigorous standards of empirical evidence. This permits them to use outrageous methods of 'proving' their hypotheses.

The baldest of these is Proof by Assertion. The author makes up for lack of facts by placing oversimplified generalizations in bold-face type or big headlines, or repeating them copiously. Much more common is Proof by Anecdote, a method also popular among journalists and politicians. Some phenomenon's appearance on earth at least once, or preferably three to five times, is cited in homey detail, with names, places, and local color. This is meant to convince the reader that similar phenomena already blanket the world, or will soon do so. Closely related is the Hyper-Extrapolated Novelty, or Exagger-Trend: a barely emergent development is projected as sure to dominate society at some unspecified future date.

When statistics appear, they are often Pseudo-Data. Thus, Mr Naisbitt says something occurs in 'as many as 80%' of the cases, which could mean anything from 1% to 80%. A more impressive anecdotal method is Global Gossip-Gathering. Specific cases of some phenomenon are cited from locations around the world to show its universality, without revealing the percentage of times it does *not* occur.

But the *tour-de-force* is Presumptive but Plausible Inter-Relatedness. This claims that many events possibly linked to some deeper underlying force area are actually caused by it, just because such linkage sounds plausible. That these phenomena might result from hundreds of other factors is left unmentioned.

This brilliant invention allows exagger-book authors to sweep dozens, even hundreds, of events and trends around the world into a few stunningly simple 'mega-trends'. For example, Mr Toffler manages to compress all human history into Three Waves. As a result, world history seems so much easier to comprehend than the reader had ever before realized! These super-simplified 'insights', though just as likely to be wrong as right, probably account for much of the enduring appeal of exagger-books. We all want to understand this bafflingly complex world, and exagger-book authors show us the way with amazing clarity.

My favorite exagger-book technique, however, is the Gradually Retracted Shocker. It is used by authors whose consciences compel them to recognize at least some hard facts – but only after they have caught the reader's eye with a startling generalization. Thus, a headline at the beginning of one of Mr Naisbitt's chapters proclaims 'The Death of Representative Democracy', but the rest of the chapter gradually reveals that representative democracy is far from dead, though it may have a bad cold. Equally misleading is Revelation by Re-labelling. The author 'discovers' long-existent traits by inventing a new name for them. Marilyn Ferguson thus hails 'networking' as evidence of a new age. But it really seems to mean people with like interests keeping in touch with each other – something practiced for centuries, and especially since the invention of the telephone.

Yet in spite of these erroneous manipulations of pseudo-facts, exagger-books continue to outsell carefully researched studies of the same subject by stupendous ratios. There must be something awfully appealing about expounding a few good insights in a fantastically exaggerated and simplistic way. If you don't believe me, you can read all about it in my new book. It's a 600-page blockbuster exposé entitled *Future Shlock: The Mega-Hype Conspiracy*. I know a good thing when I see one!

'Exagger-books' mentioned in the text

Marilyn Ferguson (1987), *The Aquarian Conspiracy: Personal and Social Transformation in the 1980s*, New York: J. P. Tarsher.

John Naisbitt (1984), *Megatrends: Ten New Directions Transforming Our Lives*, New York: Warner Books. This analysis of ten major trends foreseen by Naisbitt at that time expresses his total optimism about the future. Naisbitt never mentions a trend he doesn't like; his basic approach is to tell readers – with exaggerated enthusiasm – a lot of things they would naturally like to hear, and ignore all problems that might arise.

Vance Packard was the author of the following books, most of them out of print: *The Hidden Persuaders* (1957), an attack on modern advertising; *The Status Seekers* (1959); *The Waste Makers* (1960); *The Naked Society* (1964), on the loss of privacy in modern commercialized society; *The People Shapers* (1977).

Howard J. Ruff (1984), *How to Prosper During the Coming Bad Years*, New York: Warner Books. This book was published just before the huge economic boom years from 1985 to 1989, followed by a recession in the early 1990s that became a record expansion from 1991.

Alvin Toffler (latest edition 1991), *The Third Wave*, New York: Bantam Books. This essay condenses all human history into three waves, the biggest of which is now hitting humanity.

Alvin Toffler (1970), *Future Shock*, New York: Random House. This is an essay about how the rapid pace of change in modern life affects our lives, and how it will affect them even more radically in the future, causing an upsetting of many established traditions.

Anthony Downs

The Evolution of Democracy: How Its Axioms and Institutional Forms Have Been Adapted to Changing Social Forces

DEMOCRATIC SYSTEMS OF GOVERNMENT have always differed greatly, both because their underlying societies have varied traits, and because each democracy was established through a unique historical process. However, most major democracies in existence for more than 100 years have experienced a similar, dramatic evolution in their interpretations of democracy's three central axioms: the principles of individual liberty, equality, and citizen participation in government. This evolution in interpretation has been caused by three factors: (1) inherent ambiguities in the meaning of each axiom, (2) changes in underlying social conditions, many caused by forces common to all these democracies, and (3) ongoing interactions among the three axioms themselves. The ways in which this evolution has proceeded in long-established democracies are related to the particular institutional forms adopted by each democracy. This essay first examines the evolution of democracy's axioms, and then discusses how the institutional structure of each democracy is related to the underlying traits of its culture and population.

THE EVOLUTION OF CITIZEN PARTICIPATION

Most of the democracies established in the eighteenth and nineteenth centuries did not initially permit all adult citizens to vote; they restricted the franchise to propertied adult men. As time passed,

119

120   *Anthony Downs*

however, this interpretation of the principle of citizen participation gradually broadened. Property restrictions were slowly eliminated, permitting large groups of relatively poor male workers to vote. Then women were enfranchised.

But ending legal barriers to voting did not allow all groups in society to become politically active. In the United States, black political participation in the South was effectively inhibited for two centuries—first by slavery, then by various devices like the poll tax and threats of retaliation against freed blacks who voted. Blacks' participation in politics became relatively unconstrained only after the civil rights disturbances of the 1960s.

Recent extensions of citizen participation have gone beyond the exercise of voting rights to widespread direct political action by more groups than in the past. These include groups representing special interests, specific neighborhoods, single issues, corporations, and population segments such as homosexuals. The ability of a small number of people to obtain broad publicity for their cause by staging media events has contributed to this expansion. It has opened the way for more groups to gain power—at least the power to be consulted in government decisionmaking.

In fact, some political scientists believe citizen participation in government decisionmaking has become too widespread.[1] Greater citizen participation often causes long delays in decisionmaking because many affected groups are consulted and must take time to arrive at a mutual agreement. Because of both inflation and interest payments on committed funds, these delays can add immensely to the costs of building such proposed projects as nuclear power plants, highways, and shopping centers. In some cases, each involved group can veto any change in the status quo by withholding its approval; hence, broad citizen participation may lead to virtual paralysis. Even so, the current trend in most democracies is toward including more citizens in many decisionmaking processes.

Nevertheless, large numbers of citizens in modern democracies do not participate in governing themselves. In the United States, close to half of all eligible citizens fail to vote in major elections. Even larger fractions do not participate in politics in other ways. This situation has generated two different reactions among political observers.

One is cynicism concerning the possibility of "government with the consent of the governed." Persons with this attitude believe "citizen

The Evolution of Democracy 121

participation" is a fiction that disguises actual control of the governing process by one or more small elites; they cite data concerning the low level of political information held by most citizens in democracies to prove that most people do not want to participate intensively in politics.

The other attitude is that more and more people should be directly incorporated in the governing process. Proponents of this view hope that greater leisure time resulting from higher productivity, shorter work weeks, and a more equal distribution of income will enable more citizens to participate in politics. They believe that people will do so because of the inherent joys of political involvement and a desire to exert greater influence on government policies. Advocates of increased participation believe that it would greatly improve the character and the civic responsibility of those citizens who became more active. This change would also represent a further step toward true "government by the people."

This view of "proper" citizen participation encompasses far more direct political activity than what now occurs. Michael Walzer recognizes that expecting greatly intensified citizen participation may be unrealistic. Recalling Oscar Wilde's remark that socialism would take too many evenings, he expresses his skepticism regarding its success:

Radical politics radically increases the amount and intensity of political participation, but it does not (and probably ought not) break through the limits imposed on republican virtue by the inevitable pluralism of commitments, the terrible shortage of time, and the day-to-day hedonism of ordinary men and women. . . . Participatory democracy means the sharing of power among the activists. Socialism means the rule of the people with the most evenings to spare.[2]

Yet even this modified view of future citizen participation calls for much more widespread personal involvement in government affairs than now occurs in most democratic societies. Whether citizen participation in democracies will evolve in this direction remains to be seen.

DEVELOPMENT OF THE WELFARE STATE FROM THE EQUALITY PRINCIPLE

Broadening the scope of citizen participation had a strong impact on the interpretation of the principle of equality. As more nonpropertied

122   *Anthony Downs*

and poor persons gained potential political influence, elected politicians created more ways for national governments to improve their welfare. Eventually, a whole set of government programs emerged; together, they comprise the "welfare state." Its basic goal is to provide publicly-financed assistance to those without the means to remedy their problems of unemployment, poor health, physical disabilities, old age, or property losses caused by natural disasters.

The welfare state is an application of democracy's equality axiom. Most of its programs involve taxing people in the middle and upper portions of society's income distribution to help people in the middle and lower portions. The welfare state came into being because providing every citizen with one vote gave large numbers of lower-income people the political power to benefit themselves by heavily taxing smaller numbers of more affluent citizens. The net result has been greater equality of post-tax, post-transfer incomes among all households. In reality, much of this redistribution shifts resources from one part of the middle class to another, rather than to the lower classes. Nevertheless, considered in the aggregate within each democracy, welfare state programs—including the taxes that support them—clearly shift resources downward, thereby increasing economic equality.[3]

TENSIONS BETWEEN THE AXIOM OF INDIVIDUAL LIBERTY AND DEMOCRACY'S OTHER AXIOMS

The evolution of the equality principle's manifestations has created increased disparity between this principle and that of individual liberty. Because of inherent inequalities in abilities among individuals, operating a nation's economy through relatively free markets generally results in large income inequalities.[4] Thus, giving relatively free rein to individual liberty economically may reduce economic equality, in contrast to what obtains in more restrictive economic regimes. Conversely, increasing economic equality through development of a welfare state tends to restrict certain individual liberties. By imposing heavy taxes on high-income households, the welfare state reduces their freedom to use pre-tax resources. It also restricts freedom of entrepreneurial action by regulating minimum wage, working hours, required vacations and holidays, pensions, working conditions, and environmental pollution.

Encouragement of citizen participation, leading ever-larger shares of the population to become politically active, is not always consistent with the principle of individual liberty. On the one hand, increased citizen participation has increased the liberties of groups whose members formerly considered themselves politically powerless, such as blacks and Hispanics in the United States, and working-class residents in the United Kingdom. On the other hand, because relatively affluent citizens were the first to attain political power in early democracies, every broadening of citizen participation has weakened their power; hence their complaints that these extensions have "interfered with their liberties." Robert Moss expressed this view when he wrote:

The apparatus of the Welfare State has extended far beyond its original goals, which were accepted by all parties: the creation of real equality of opportunity and the provision for the basic necessities of people who are unable (because of age, or infirmity, or the hazards of economic life) to fend for themselves. The Welfare State has instead become a means of shielding its beneficiaries from every risk that is likely to confront them between cradle and coffin.[5]

Moss believes these extensions of government power are detrimental; he states that "there no longer appear to be accepted or enforceable limits to government action, which is steadily cutting away the social and economic basis for a free society."[6] Yet studies of the distribution of incomes and wealth in most democratic societies show conclusively that households in the upper 20 percent of every such society still control disproportionately large shares of economic resources, while those in the lower 20 percent have disproportionately small shares.[7] The welfare state's "interference" with the individual liberties of the affluent has not resulted in anything like the establishment of economic equality.

THE EVOLUTION OF THE PRINCIPLE OF INDIVIDUAL LIBERTY

The meaning of individual liberty has evolved in conflicting directions. Individual rights to use private property have been increasingly restricted in the twentieth century by expanding government powers and regulations, including adoption of a progressive income tax and passage of laws limiting entrepreneurial actions. Most of these restrictions have been justified as necessary for the protection of citizens from adverse consequences of individual or corporate actions. For example, laws require businesses to clean up harmful environmental spills to protect innocent bystanders from pollution.

At the same time, the rights of individuals at the bottom of society have been expanded in two ways. The welfare state is designed to reduce the inherent risks of life by providing basic benefits to those who cannot afford them. Some of these benefits, such as health care and food stamps, have become "rights" in the sense that everyone in society with certain attributes is entitled to receive them.

In the United States, the noneconomic rights of individuals have been notably expanded in the past few decades. The civil rights of ethnic minorities are now given greater legislative and administrative protection than in the past. In addition, persons accused of crimes must be informed of their rights upon arrest, provided with counsel, protected from searches without warrants, and given decent living conditions if jailed. In general, the evolution of individual rights in democracies during the past century has moved toward their expansion rather than their contraction, in spite of greater restrictions on the use of property.

THE MULTIPLE DIMENSIONS OF EQUALITY IN SOCIETY

The principle of equality is hard to define because the situations and capabilities of individuals within every society are diverse and hence unequal.[8] As Douglas Rae has said, "Specific notions of equality are spawned from the general idea of equality, and come into conflict with one another. Perhaps indeed the idea against which equality must struggle most heroically is equality itself."[9] A few examples of the paradox revealed in Rae's analysis are worth considering.

Should equality be conceived of as person-regarding or lot-regarding? The former means providing conditions that are equally well tailored to the varied and subjective needs, conditions, and capabilities of every individual. Policies designed to achieve this must treat each person differently, in accordance with his or her specific circumstances. In contrast, lot-regarding equality provides each person with equal, objective allocations. In education, for example, person-regarding equality would involve many different educational programs tailored to suit the talents and interests of each child; lot-regarding equality would provide each child with exactly the same courses and materials.

Lot-regarding equality has the advantage of being publicly demonstrable while requiring no attention to the traits of individual subjects. The achievement of person-regarding equality requires comparing immeasurable subjective mental states of individual satisfaction, or at least taking the varying traits of individuals into account. Some public policies, such as paying for health care, do respond to individuals' specific needs for aid by treating those with different perceived needs differently (but treating those with the same perceived needs equally). Yet while person-regarding equality is what matters most to human beings, public policies usually focus on lot-regarding equality because it is much easier to administer.

To whom should equality apply? Within a given population, should it be inclusionary (applying to everyone in the population) or exclusionary (applying only to subgroups of the entire population)? A common example of exclusionary application involves dividing society into segments according to certain traits, treating all individuals within each segment equally, but treating people within different segments differently. For instance, low-income women who head households with children are eligible for federal aid for families with dependent children; presumably, women within this group have equal access to such aid. But women who head households with children and have higher incomes are not eligible; nor are single men. Any intensive division of labor creates multiple grounds for social segmentation of this type, which is almost universal.

Trying to achieve inclusionary equality throughout a large society—in respect, for example, to education or incomes—has a negative effect on individual liberties in the sense that it usually requires strong centralization of power. If power is decentralized, however, and given to subgroups, no one can ensure that members of different subgroups are treated equally. Therefore, the more traits one believes should be equalized for everyone in society, the more one is committed to supporting centralized government power. Clearly, the principle of equality can conflict with the principle of individual liberty.

Finally, to what domains should equality apply, and what specific elements of a given domain should be equalized? Consider the broad domain of economic resources. In all large societies, both total wealth

126   *Anthony Downs*

and pre-tax incomes are unequal. Should income tax rates be made equal for all to achieve marginal equality? That policy would cover only a narrow portion of all economic resources; it would fail to produce equality in the broader domain of after-tax incomes. Persons with high pre-tax incomes would still have much greater after-tax incomes than persons with low pre-tax incomes. Should after-tax incomes be made equal for all? Even if that were done (through unequal marginal tax rates), great inequality would remain within a still broader domain: total wealth. Should total wealth be made equal for all, to create a "global equality" of economic resources? That would require massively unequal redistributions of wealth through government coercion. Yet these redistributions could be considered compensatory inequality: distributing a good unequally in order to offset a preexisting inequality.[10]

Broadening the domain within which equality is sought increases the need for centralized government power to attain it. Choosing how narrow or how broad that domain should be is a major issue in most democracies today. An additional complication is that different domains may be linked causally; equalizing (or failing to equalize) in one domain can affect how equal things will be in another. For example, while capitalist economic theory advocates rewarding people equally in relation to their individual productivity, that productivity is influenced by unequally distributed factors such as education and inherited talents.

Other complexities concerning applications of the principle of equality include the following:

• Most egalitarian public policies try to attain greater relative equality rather than absolute equality. The former implies that one allocation of resources will be closer to complete equality than another, but neither will ever achieve it. The latter implies that there will be complete equality among individuals in the overall distribution of the resource concerned.

• Should public policies aim at equality of opportunity or equality of result? The former implies that every individual will have an equal chance of attaining some outcome, but doing so will depend on individual ability or effort. The latter implies that every individual involved will attain exactly the same outcome regardless of personal traits.

The Evolution of Democracy   127

Applying the principle of equality in practice involves grappling with difficult issues, not the least being the conflicts among individuals who subscribe to different meanings of that principle. It is scarcely surprising that great inequalities continue to exist within societies that sincerely espouse the principle of equality.

WHICH SPECIFIC RIGHTS SHOULD BE CONSIDERED "INALIENABLE"?

There is no widespread agreement as to which specific rights should be considered inalienable in a democracy. The Declaration of Independence identified such rights as including (but not necessarily limited to) "life, liberty, and the pursuit of happiness." The Bill of Rights enumerated more specific rights, including the right to freedom of speech, religion, and assembly, to a jury trial by one's peers, and to private property.[11] More recently, the American Roman Catholic bishops declared that such rights should include decent housing, adequate health care, and a minimum-wage job.[12]

Most of the specific rights enumerated in the Declaration of Independence and the U.S. Constitution were designed to allow individuals to act on their own behalf, or as they see fit, without undue interference from the government. Those rights do not entitle individuals to specific outcomes—only to the opportunity to act. The Declaration of Independence does not say that individuals have the right to "happiness" (something that no government can guarantee), but only to "the pursuit of happiness." The responsibility for achieving specific outcomes is left to each individual; this approach assumes that every citizen possesses some degree of self-reliance.

In contrast, some people today argue that every citizen has an inalienable right to certain material outcomes, such as decent housing and adequate health care. They contend that if an individual cannot achieve those outcomes (as many cannot), society should provide them. This approach raises four key issues:

•*Exactly how should these material outcomes be defined?* For example, what constitutes "decent" housing? To be considered decent, just how big must a housing unit be, how well-built must it be, what specific amenities (such as heating, plumbing, water, electricity, garage, air-conditioning) must it contain, how crowded can it be, and in what kind of a neighborhood must it be located? At present, answers to these questions vary immensely throughout the world. Should everyone in the world nevertheless be entitled to the same result? Or should acceptable standards of housing decency vary from one society to another, or even within different parts of a society?

• *Who should pay for provision of material outcomes to those who cannot achieve them on their own?* The financial resources required may be very large indeed, especially if such rights are to be provided for every human being in the world. But who must sacrifice resources they would otherwise control in order to achieve these rights on behalf of those who lack self-reliance?

• *How much authority and power should be given to governments to provide those material outcomes? And would the resulting concentration of power in governments excessively inhibit the freedom of individuals?* Experience proves that the voluntary efforts of private citizens are insufficient to provide material outcomes to all persons who cannot achieve such outcomes themselves. Instead, governments typically must assume much of that responsibility; they must use either explicit or implicit coercion (usually through taxes) to take resources away from some people to provide others with these outcomes. This process expands the power of government at the expense of the rights and material well-being of many citizens. How far can such expansion of government power go without endangering other elements of democracy?

• *Should receipt of these material outcomes be an inalienable right of all human beings on earth, or just of citizens within the society thus defining such rights?* Individual rights are meaningless in practice unless institutions exist that are both capable of carrying them out and willing to do so. At present, nation-states are the major institutions that fill this role, and they tend to pay more attention to the rights of their own citizens than to those of citizens in other nation-states. This is true in both defining individual rights and in enforcing them. What moral obligation does each society have to extend the material outcomes implied by "inalienable rights" to all other persons elsewhere? And how could it do so without infringing on the powers of governments in other nation-states?

There are no unequivocal answers to these questions that are equally applicable in all times, places, and societies. The achievement

The Evolution of Democracy   129

and definition of humanity's "inalienable" individual rights appear to be the results of gradual historical processes. Three dimensions of individual rights are still evolving: (1) recognition of the basic idea of their inalienability; (2) specific definition of what rights should be considered inalienable; and (3) extension of their actual achievement to more and more people.

Throughout most of human history, governments have not maintained that every individual possesses inalienable rights. While certain individual rights were accorded citizens in ancient Greece, the Roman Empire, and other societies, these rights were not considered inalienable, and many people were denied them. The concept of inalienability of individual rights owes something to the Christian belief that all people are created by God with immortal souls and opportunity for personal salvation. But the concept of inalienable rights became widely recognized in practice only after the Declaration of Independence, and even the Founding Fathers did not extend such rights to slaves or women. To achieve that took over 130 years, requiring both a bloody civil war and several constitutional amendments. In certain respects, the achievement of basic political rights for most American citizens, regardless of race or sex, is still not fully guaranteed.

The current attempt to extend the concept of inalienable rights from the mainly political rights conceived of by the Founding Fathers to the economic rights espoused by the Catholic bishops (but not yet accepted by the U.S. Congress) can be seen as part of this process of evolution. This is also true of the U.S. government's attempts to make human rights issues part of its foreign policy, and of certain private groups' efforts to pressure governments throughout the world to end torture and arbitrary imprisonment.[13] In each of these cases, some group is trying to extend the currently accepted boundaries of one of the three dimensions of individual rights. There is likely to be a never-ending struggle between those who seek to extend those boundaries and those who wish to maintain them or constrict them to narrower areas of application.

TWO PROTOTYPES FOR THE FORMS OF DEMOCRATIC GOVERNMENTS

While democratic governments are compelled to deal with such issues, how they do so will be fundamentally affected by the kinds of

1 3 0   *Anthony Downs*

political institutions they have adopted. The multitude of democratic forms can be analyzed in relationship to two basic prototypes.[14] Both embody all the central axioms of democracy, but each emphasizes a different one. These two prototypes represent two different answers to the question: What is meant by *the people* in the fundamental definition of democracy as "government by the people"? As Arend Lijphart asked, "Who will do the governing and to whose interests should the government be responsive when the people are in disagreement and have divergent preferences?" He goes on to say:

> One answer is: the majority of the people. Its great merit is that any other answer, such as the requirement of unanimity or a qualified majority, entails minority rule—or at least a minority veto—and that government by the majority and in accordance with the majority's wishes comes closer to the democratic ideal than government by and responsive to a minority.[15]

This answer leads to the *majoritarian model* of democracy. Its institutions emphasize majority rule, which is derived from the central principle of equality.

But there is another equally compelling answer: government should be responsive to as many people as possible. W. Arthur Lewis has argued that the primary meaning of democracy is that "all who are affected by a decision should have the chance to participate in making that decision, either directly or through chosen representatives."[16] If a majority wins office in a democracy and does not allow the minority to exercise any power in government, then those excluded are not truly participating in self-government.

The merit of the latter answer is that a government that responds to nearly all sizable groups in society to some degree does not leave any minorities feeling left out or neglected. Hence it is less likely to spawn resentment and disloyalty from minority groups than a government that serves only a majority. This idea leads to the *consensual model* of democracy, whose institutions emphasize citizen participation, one of the central principles of democracy.

The majoritarian and consensual prototypes can be viewed as two contrasting models in a broad spectrum of possible democratic institutions. Analysis of these models illuminates possible underlying relationships between the democratic institutions in a society and its key social and cultural conditions.

The Evolution of Democracy   131

The Majoritarian Prototype

Majoritarian institutional forms concentrate governmental powers in the hands of whatever party wins the most votes, excluding other parties from any exercise of power whatsoever. They also concentrate government powers in the national legislature and especially in the executive derived from that legislature. Little power is delegated to lower-level bodies such as state, province, or local governments. Moreover, there are no external checks on the power of the legislature, such as judicial review of its actions.

As developed by Lijphart, the majoritarian prototype in its purest form contains the following basic elements:

• Concentration of executive power through one-party and bare-majority cabinets in the government.

• Fusion of power within the executive cabinet through strong cabinet dominance of government.

• A two-house legislature in which one house has most of the power.

• A two-party system.

• A largely one-dimensional party system in which political contests and governmental issues focus on a single major dimension (e.g., socioeconomic policies in the United Kingdom).

• A plurality system of election in which the party with the most votes wins office, and all others are excluded from office. This is usually accompanied by single-member electoral districts in which the individual candidate with the most votes is the sole person elected from each district.

• Unitary and centralized government, with dominant power exercised at the national level rather than at lower levels (i.e., state, province, or local governments).

• No written constitution.

• Parliamentary sovereignty: all final power is vested in the legislature, with no formal judicial review of its decisions.

• Exclusively representative democracy: no direct votes on issues by the citizenry.

Only a few governments actually exhibit all these characteristics. Lijphart cites New Zealand and the United Kingdom as coming closest to this prototype; many others have most of these traits.

132   *Anthony Downs*

There are big differences between the presidential and parliamentary forms of the majoritarian model. In the presidential system, used in the United States, the executive and legislature are separately elected. In the parliamentary system, only the legislature is elected; its members then select key members of the executive. The executive is more powerful in the parliamentary system because its members can normally count on support from a majority in the legislature. But the executive is more stable in the presidential system because the legislature cannot dismiss it from office.

The concentration of power in majoritarian systems usually gives the government the ability to act decisively. It also permits relatively strong coordination of governmental policies throughout the society. But the exclusion of minority groups from exercising governmental power may alienate them from the government or even from the whole political system. Whether this occurs depends greatly on how strongly differences among social groups influence their thinking and behavior.

If the society's population is relatively homogeneous in its major traits, the beliefs and policy preferences of all sizable segments do not differ dramatically; therefore, no segment fears governmental dominance by any other. Similar confidence is encouraged if the society's key political controversies involve a single "issue dimension." For example, the biggest perennial political battles in the United Kingdom concern economic issues: how incomes should be taxed and redistributed, how many government resources should be devoted to social services, and whether or not the government should own any of the major means of production. Little political energy is devoted to religious or cultural–ethnic questions, urban–rural conflicts, and other issues that are divisive in other democratic societies.

The Consensual Prototype

Many societies are sharply divided into subgroups with widely varying beliefs about what society ought to be like and what policies governments ought to adopt. Such social cleavages can occur in respect to many issues, including those of a socioeconomic, religious, cultural–ethnic, and urban–rural nature; degrees of loyalty or hostility to democracy; attitudes about foreign policy; and attitudes about political participation and environmentalism.

In cleavage-ridden societies, exclusion of large groups from governmental power may represent a threat to those groups. They may fear that permitting another group to exercise great governmental power could result in policies harmful to their preferred way of life or even to their survival as a group. Such fears can weaken their allegiance to democratic forms of government. As Robert Dahl has pointed out, "Any dispute in which a large section of the population of a country feels that its way of life or its highest values are severely menaced by another segment of the population creates a crisis in a competitive system."[17] For example, in parts of India, many Sikhs appear to be rejecting democracy because the government is dominated by Hindus, who they fear will not allow them sufficient religious freedom. Such outcomes can be avoided by permitting sizable minority groups to share enough governmental power so that they do not fear that the government will harm their vital interests. This requires that minorities have both (1) a significant voice in shaping current government policies and (2) enough power to prevent major changes in existing policies to which they had agreed at the outset of democratic government. These objectives can be achieved through institutional forms designed to restrain the majority's governmental powers. Such forms comprise the consensual prototype of democracy, which requires the majority to share, fairly distribute, disperse, delegate, and limit its exercise of governmental powers. Its basic elements are as follows:

- Sharing of executive power in grand coalitions containing members of all major political parties, including those with minority shares of the total vote. At least some positions are thus assigned to every party with any significant percentage of the total vote, except for extremist parties (those opposed to democracy itself).

- Separation of powers within different parts of the government (legislative, executive, and judicial), both formally and informally.

- A two-house legislature in which both houses exercise about-equal powers, but one gives minorities special representation disproportionate to their absolute numbers in society.

- A multiparty system in which each party is usually identified with specific subgroups in society.

1 3 4   *Anthony Downs*

- A multiple-dimension party system in which political contests and government policies are not focused on a single set of issues, but involve several dimensions (such as the distribution of income among different socioeconomic groups, and linkages of public policies to specific religious or ethnic viewpoints).

- Proportional representation, in which each party (either at the national or district level) elects persons to office roughly in proportion to its share of the overall vote, rather than by winning a plurality of votes.

- Territorial and nonterritorial federalism and decentralization, in which significant governmental powers are formally vested in bodies below the national level, such as provinces, states, or localities.

- A written constitution that provides a minority with the ability to veto changes in it.

   In contrast to the majoritarian prototype, the consensual model is designed to concentrate less power in the hands of the majority. Minority members can hold office within the national executive branch, win office and exercise significant power at lower levels of government, be represented in the legislature in proportion to their share of the total vote, and veto changes in the written constitution. Thus, within a consensual system, groups too small to form a majority can nevertheless participate meaningfully in the processes of government, and can even block major changes in existing governmental policies. The consensual prototype may be a far more effective form of democracy than the majoritarian prototype in pluralistic societies containing major social or other cleavages.

   Lijphart believes that Switzerland is the only government that embodies nearly every element of the pure form of consensual government. Belgium, Finland, and the Netherlands, however, also have governments dominated by consensual elements.

FACTORS AFFECTING RELATIONSHIPS BETWEEN SOCIAL CONDITIONS AND DEMOCRATIC FORMS

The above discussion indicates that—at least in theory—there ought to be important relationships between the basic conditions prevalent

The Evolution of Democracy   135

in any democratic society and the specific forms of its governmental institutions. Societies with relatively homogeneous populations seem best suited for majoritarian institutions, whereas pluralistic societies containing many subgroups with diverse but intensely-held beliefs seem best suited for consensual institutions. But an examination of actual relationships between fundamental social conditions and democratic institutional forms shows these generalizations to be oversimplified. What variable social conditions are most relevant to determining which democratic forms might work best in each society?

Different Levels of Intensity Concerning Political Issues

Nearly all societies contain sizable subgroups with different characteristics and viewpoints. One factor determining the importance of these differences to democratic government is the intensity with which specific subgroups hold certain views or beliefs. This can be illustrated by a comparison of different levels of intensity concerning socioeconomic and religious issues—just two of several possible issue dimensions.

Socioeconomic issues relate to how much the government regulates, modifies, or controls economic markets. Specifically, they concern the following policy questions:[18]

- Governmental (versus private) ownership of the means of production.
- A strong (versus weak) governmental role in economic planning.
- Support of (versus opposition to) the redistribution of wealth from the rich to the poor.
- Expansion of (versus resistance to) governmental social welfare programs.

Two expert observers have reached seemingly opposite conclusions about the saliency of these questions in democratic politics. Lijphart found that the socioeconomic dimension was present in all twenty-two democratic governments he analyzed, and was a central political issue in nineteen of them (all but Canada, Iceland, and the United States).* The second most common issue dimension was

---

*Lijphart analyzed twenty-one democratic *nations*, but twenty-two democratic *governments*, since he counted the Fourth and Fifth Republics in France separately. In most cases, I will refer to twenty-two democracies.

136 *Anthony Downs*

religion, present in eleven democracies and a high-saliency issue in nine of them. No other issue dimensions were nearly as important within these democracies.[19]

But Robert Dahl argues that socioeconomic differences, in contrast to religious differences, have almost never fragmented societies into "warring groups":

> For over a century, reflections about polarizations and civil war have been dominated, even among non-Marxists, by Marx's conception of polarization around the node of economic classes—working class and bourgeoisie. Yet ... since the Communist Manifesto was published, no country has developed according to the Marxist model of conflict, nor has any regime, whether hegemonic or competitive, fallen or been transformed because of a clear-cut polarization of working class and bourgeoisie.[20]

Dahl concludes that major social cleavages are more likely to be based on differences in religion, language, race or ethnic group, and region than on economic class conflicts. These bases of fragmentation are more profound and longer-lasting than economic issues:

> Presumably because an ethnic or religious identity is incorporated so early and so deeply into one's personality, conflicts among ethnic or religious sub-cultures are specially fraught with danger, particularly if they are also tied to region. . . . Conflicts among ethnic and religious sub-cultures are so easily seen as threats to one's fundamental self.[21]

The seemingly contradictory conclusions of Lijphart and Dahl are not inconsistent if a society can deal with controversial issues on two separate levels.[22] One level is the arena of electoral political conflict, in which decisions are made through the voting process and subsequent government action. The losing parties in this arena must accept policy changes made by the winners (who may be just a bare majority) through normal legislative and executive action.

Another, deeper level is in the society's fundamental political constitution, whether written or unwritten. The constitution embodies institutional and policy arrangements considered too important to be dealt with in the normal electoral manner. A social consensus exists (usually explicit in written constitutions) that society cannot change these constitutional structures without going through extraordinary processes that are deliberately made difficult to carry out. More than a bare majority of voters is almost always required to approve of proposed constitutional changes.

The Evolution of Democracy 137

These two levels are related to what Bruce Berkowitz has called "pivotal issues" in his theory of political stability.[23] In many societies, certain groups—often minorities—consider key existing social arrangements critically important to their welfare. They do not want changes in those arrangements to be possible through normal electoral processes that might be controlled by a bare majority. In fact, many members of such groups are willing to remain peaceful citizens of the existing democracy only as long as these key arrangements remain unchanged. To gain their support in the initial formation of the political order, framers of the basic constitution embed these arrangements in the constitution itself, outside the arena of common political controversy.

Berkowitz believes that slavery was a pivotal issue in the development of the American Constitution. To gain the support of southern states, the Constitution of 1789 did not challenge the continuation of slavery, in spite of sweeping rhetoric about the sanctity of human rights that appears in both the Constitution and the preceding Declaration of Independence. Later, American public opinion changed enough to make slavery's continuance a major issue in the normal political arena. As a result, the South quit the Union rather than accept the antislavery policies that seemed imminent. It took the bloodiest war in American history to restore southern membership to the Union under the revised Constitution.

In considering how powerfully an issue causing social cleavage may affect democracy, it is necessary to examine at what level of intensity or profundity that issue exists in the minds of its proponents. Lijphart found that "socioeconomic status, or social class, is of universal importance in virtually all industrialized countries, and . . . religion is often not important at all, such as in religiously homogeneous societies; however, *when both factors play a role, religion tends to have a stronger influence on party choice* [on voting behavior].[24] (Italics added.)

This observation indicates that when voters regard religion as politically important, they view it as more profoundly important than socioeconomic issues. Yet Lijphart also found that when both socioeconomic and religious issues were present in a democratic system, socioeconomic factors were far more important in determining how political parties combined to form coalition governments.[25] But coalition governments function mainly at the level of normal electoral politics, whereas religious issues are more likely to be dealt with at the deeper constitutional level. Taking the two levels into account reconciles these seemingly conflicting findings.

Intensity of Group Loyalties

How strongly members of a given group feel loyal to that group or to its principles can greatly influence their political behavior. This introduces potentially powerful nonrational elements into that behavior.[26] The intensity of such loyalties can change markedly over time, and varies tremendously from one place to another. For example, religious conflicts between Catholics and Protestants stimulated centuries of bitter warfare throughout Europe after the Reformation. But the growth of secularism and the development of religious freedom within Western societies have greatly diminished the influence of Christian religious beliefs on politics. Such beliefs no longer engender much political and social conflict (except in a few locations, such as Ireland). On the other hand, religious beliefs remain strong political forces in much of the Islamic world; their importance has increased dramatically during the past two decades in Pakistan, Indonesia, Iran, and other parts of the Middle East.

Whether Divisive Factors are "Reinforcing" or "Crosscutting"[27]

Different divisive factors, such as religion and economic status, are reinforcing if most members of one group concerning one factor (e.g., Protestants concerning religion) are also members of one group concerning another factor (e.g., wealthy or middle-class individuals concerning economic status), while most members of some other group concerning the first factor (Catholics) are also members of some other group concerning the second factor (poor). In such cases, the separateness and possible antipathy of each group vis-à-vis the other concerning religion is strengthened by their matching separateness concerning economic status.

Divisive factors are crosscutting if members of one group concerning one factor (e.g., Protestants) are divided among several different groups concerning a second factor (e.g., wealthy, middle-class, poor) rather than all similar in regard to that factor, while members of a second group (Catholics) are also divided among several groups concerning that second factor. In this example, the separateness of Protestants and Catholics concerning religion is partly offset by the

The Evolution of Democracy 139

fact that both Protestants and Catholics belong to several different economic status groups, each such group containing both Protestant and Catholic members who presumably share similar viewpoints concerning economic status.

Societies in which many divisive factors are reinforcing are likely to have more severe social cleavages than those in which most divisive factors are crosscutting. As Seymour Martin Lipset explains, "Multiple and politically inconsistent affiliations, loyalties, and stimuli reduce the emotion and aggressiveness involved in political choice. . . . The chances for stable democracy are enhanced to the extent that groups and individuals have a number of crosscutting, politically relevant affiliations."[28] For example, in the United States, Catholics and Protestants generally have similar educational attainments and income and occupational distributions, and belong to many of the same groups concerning nonreligious factors. Any likely political impacts of their religious differences are muted by their joint membership in these other groups. In contrast, most Chinese citizens in Malaysia are also Buddhist and relatively well-off economically; most Malays are also Moslem and relatively poor. These triply-reinforcing divisions have created a deep cleavage between the two groups.

The Balance of Power Among Divided Groups

The political impact of deep cleavages among social subgroups is immensely influenced by the relative overall strength of each subgroup. In societies where one subgroup is much larger than all others and commands more resources, the distribution of political power will be quite different from that in societies where several major subgroups have roughly the same size and resources. For example, in Singapore, persons of Chinese ancestry account for most of the population, although members of many other ethnic groups are present. Hence the Chinese are politically dominant, even though they permit three other languages to be used in Singapore schools. But in Lebanon, dozens of different religious sects (often with ethnically homogeneous members) are present, and none of them is able to dominate all the others. Their relative parity has aggravated the amount of conflict in that society.

Robert Dahl contends that societies containing just two major social groups are more likely to be gripped by intense political conflict than those containing many social groups, none of which constitutes a majority. In a society with only two major social groups, one group is a majority and the other a minority; the latter may feel threatened by a government dominated by the former, especially if the minority seems perpetually condemned to being out of power. Northern Ireland exemplifies this situation. But in a multigroup society in which no one group can completely dominate, groups are more likely to cooperate in order to aggregate enough power to accomplish common goals. Dahl cites India as an example of this situation.[29]

The Geographic Location of Different Subgroups

If most members of a certain group are concentrated in a single area of a nation, and if that area's population consists primarily of those members, the area is likely to press for considerable autonomy in its own affairs. Members of the concentrated group may even seek independence from the nation. Such pressure is clearly visible today among the Basques in Spain, the Tamils in Sri Lanka, the Sikhs in parts of India. However, geographic concentration of a minority also makes it possible to create a federal system of government in which considerable power is delegated to local residents. Such strong federalism is difficult or impossible when members of each minority are scattered geographically, with members of many different groups commingled in each area.

Total Size of the Nation

The larger a nation's population, the harder it is to achieve unity among its members. Large nations are more likely to contain heterogeneous ethnic groups than small nations are. Moreover, differing regional perspectives are more likely to have developed over time within big nations. Consequently, large countries are more likely to adopt federal systems that decentralize power. Also, G. Bingham Powell, Jr., found population size positively related to political rioting and deaths.[30] Perhaps the remoteness from government felt by average citizens in a large nation predisposes them to seek meaningful participation through violence rather than through more legitimate channels.

Prior Traditional Relationships Among Elites

Democracy requires a certain degree of trust among leaders of all major social groups. Leaders must not fear that other groups, if they gain power, will act in a hostile manner toward them or their groups. Whether such attitudes of reciprocal trust and tolerance exist among leadership elites in a society is determined by their past relationships. For example, in some African nations, neighboring tribes have long histories of bitter warfare in which each tribe has murdered thousands of the other tribe's members. Such relationships are hardly a foundation for stable democracy in a newly-independent nation.

THE IMPORTANCE OF SPECIFIC CONSTITUTIONAL AND ELECTORAL FORMS IN DEMOCRACY

Recent empirical studies prove that specific constitutional and electoral forms are not the only major determinants of government behavior in democracies. Moreover, causality often flows two ways: a society's specific institutional forms influence its political behavior, but its underlying social traits may also influence its initial choice of institutional forms. The latter relationship is vital in considering what forms might be best suited to presently nondemocratic societies if and when they consider becoming democracies.

Electoral and Party Systems

Two key aspects of democratic institutions are how governments are elected and how many major parties the political system contains. These aspects are closely related because each type of electoral system generates a specific type of party system.

One of the two commonly used methods of choosing a government is electing a single representative from each geographic district. The candidate who gets the most votes is chosen; all others are rejected. Use of such single-member district representation emphasizes winning a plurality of votes in each area; the only sure way to do that is to win a majority. Therefore, in the nation as a whole, small interest groups have a powerful incentive to merge into parties large enough and broad enough in appeal that they have the potential to capture a majority of votes in each district. This is why nations that elect candidates from single-member districts usually have two-party systems. Six of the twenty-two democracies analyzed by Lijphart used some type of majority or plurality electoral system; he calculated an average of 2.4 effective parties in each of these nations.[31]

142   *Anthony Downs*

This electoral system is philosophically congruent with the majoritarian approach to democracy, as it awards all governmental power to whichever candidate wins the most votes. But the majority party tends to be overrepresented in the national legislature in relation to its share of the total popular vote. This occurs because the losing minority voters in each district are, in effect, not represented at all in the legislature, even though they may comprise a significant fraction of the district's total popular vote. This electoral arrangement is found in most majoritarian systems of government. For example, in the recent British election, the Conservatives won only 42 percent of the popular vote, but they have a large majority in the House of Commons.

The other widely used method of choosing a government is electing several representatives from each district and dividing them among major parties in rough proportion to their shares of the popular vote there. Such proportional representation can be carried out in several ways.[32] All tend to generate multiparty systems because minority parties can gain representation in the national legislature even if they do not win a majority or plurality of votes in any district. Proportional representation is most often associated with parliamentary governments rather than presidential ones.[33] Fifteen of the twenty-two democracies analyzed by Lijphart used proportional representation; they averaged 3.8 effective parties per nation.[34]

Proportional representation and multiparty systems are philosophically congruent with the consensual approach to democracy because they provide means for nonmajority groups to participate directly in government. Such participation can occur through representation in the legislature and representation in the executive when coalition governments are formed.

HOW CLOSE ARE ACTUAL DEMOCRACIES TO THE TWO MAJOR PROTOTYPES?

To answer this question, Lijphart studied the twenty-one societies he considered to be reasonably stable democracies as of 1980. His factor analysis revealed that their characteristics clustered around two factors: (1) the effective number of parties,[35] and (2) attributes of federalism, including bicameralism, decentralization, and rigid constitutions. He divided the twenty-one democracies into three groups

The Evolution of Democracy   143

according to their traits related to each factor: those with clearly majoritarian traits, those with clearly consensual traits, and those with traits intermediate between majoritarian and consensual. He then developed a nine-cell matrix based on relationships between these two factors, as shown below. Societies he considered basically pluralist (as opposed to homogeneous) are shown in italics.

Classification of Democratic Systems by Arend Lijphart

Number-of-Parties Dimension	Federalism Dimension		
	Majoritarian (Centralized)	Intermediate	Consensual (Decentralized)
Majoritarian (Two Parties)	New Zealand United Kingdom	Ireland	Australia *Austria Canada Germany United States*
Intermediate	Iceland *Luxembourg*	*France V* Norway Sweden	*Italy* Japan
Consensual (Many Parties)	Denmark *Israel*	*Belgium Finland* France IV *Netherlands*	*Switzerland*

NOTE: France appears twice, for the Fourth and Fifth Republics.
Copyright © 1984 by Yale University Press. Reprinted by permission.[36]

Societies embodying the "purest" majoritarian traits are in the upper left-hand corner; those with the "purest" consensual traits are in the lower right-hand corner. Thus, only three of the twenty-one societies exhibit "pure" traits of either prototype. The largest group in any cell consists of the five societies in the upper right-hand corner. They combine consensual traits concerning federalism (that is, decentralized power structures) with majoritarian traits concerning elections (that is, less than three effective parties). Another large group (in the lowest central cell) combines intermediate decentralization of power with consensual party systems.

Actual democratic practice does not conform closely to the two "pure" prototypes; most societies mix either intermediate or opposite

144   *Anthony Downs*

traits. Yet there is a notable association of pluralist societies with consensual traits. Of the thirteen societies Lijphart considered pluralist, eleven have consensual traits concerning at least one factor, and none are "purely" majoritarian. Also, all of the democracies with Anglo-American heritage have strongly majoritarian electoral systems, whereas most Continental European democracies (eleven out of thirteen) have either consensual or intermediate electoral systems.

IS "POLITICAL DEVELOPMENT INTO NATIONHOOD" A NECESSARY PREREQUISITE TO DEMOCRACY?

Many nondemocratic societies—especially those created from former European colonies—have highly heterogeneous populations marked by deep cleavages among hostile subgroups. Some political scientists believe these societies must go through a process of "political development into nationhood" before they can possibly become effective democracies. This process has been described as follows:

Democratization and other dimensions of [political] development are usually thought to be dependent upon national integration. . . . Nation-building must be accorded priority and must be the first task of the leaders of the developing states. . . . The usual view is that nation-building entails the eradication of primordial subnational attachments and their replacement with national loyalty.[37]

Thus, greater homogeneity of views, values, and loyalties must be created among the diverse citizens of these societies before democracy can work there. Meanwhile, say some observers, such societies must remain under nondemocratic governments.

Lijphart disputes this conclusion. He argues that diverse and heterogeneous societies can become successful democracies if they adopt consensual forms designed to involve diverse groups in active government participation. Moreover, says Lijphart, it is both difficult and undesirable to end or even reduce people's loyalties to various subgroups in many societies, as these loyalties are deeply rooted in individuals' personalities and identities. Even in the United States, which has been a democracy for over 200 years, some subgroup loyalties are amazingly persistent. Despite the metaphor of the "melting pot," many American ethnic and religious groups (e.g.,

[handwritten margin note: But is begon from a homogeneous community]

The Evolution of Democracy　145

Jews, blacks, and Chinese) have maintained strong group identities over long periods.

Lijphart believes that leaders in many nondemocratic societies err in waiting until they have created a socially homogeneous population before trying democracy. They should instead design democratic institutions along consensual lines, building on strong subgroup identities rather than attempting to minimize or eliminate them.

While Lijphart is correct in contending that some pluralistic nations could erect successful democracies without destroying their social and cultural diversity, his analysis overlooks another crucial factor: the self-interest of the government elites in these nations. Most former European colonies that became independent states after World War II have abandoned their initial democratic institutional forms in favor of some type of one-party government. A key reason is that the elites who assumed power at the end of colonialism—or others who replaced them—found it advantageous to end democracy. By doing so, they consolidated their power and reduced the probability that they would be replaced in a popular election.

If these elites had tried to retain democratic institutions, they would have found themselves in a serious dilemma. Many had gained power through independence movements that generated high citizen expectations of rapid economic development, yet their societies had extremely limited capability to achieve those expectations. As the passage of time has clearly proved, these leaders were almost certain to disappoint their followers in terms of economic development. A disgruntled democratic electorate would most likely have voted them out of office, no matter how competently they had governed. To avoid that outcome, most leaders of emerging nations transformed their systems from nascent democracies into one-party states in which voters had no choice about who was running the government.

CONCLUSION

All human societies constantly change over time, and their average rate of change has accelerated dramatically during the past 200 years. Yet this period has also been the only one in human history during which democracy was widely adopted as a basic form of government. Therefore, its supporters have had to be flexible in two ways in order for democracy to survive.

146   *Anthony Downs*

One is by greatly altering the ways in which the three basic axioms of democracy have been interpreted over time as social conditions have evolved (partly in response to democracy itself). Those interpretations are still changing today.

The other is by designing specific institutional forms for democracy that vary greatly from one society to another. That permits democracy's forms to be well adapted to the particular social and geographic conditions of each society.

Both types of flexibility have been accomplished without destroying the basic nature of democracy. In fact, they can be seen as striving over time to achieve its basic ideals more fully, in a greater variety of circumstances.

This proves that democracy is a dynamic process of governance and even of living in general, not a static institutional construct. Supporters of democracy must continue to change its specific meanings and forms, without destroying its fundamental nature, if they want it to survive another 200 years.

ENDNOTES

This paper is adapted, with permission, from part of an untitled manuscript slated for future publication by The Brookings Institution, Washington, DC. Copyright © by the Brookings Institution.

[1] For example, Bernard Berelson, Paul Lazarsfeld, and William McPhee wrote as follows: "Lack of interest by some people is not without its benefits. . . . Extreme interest goes with extreme partisanship and might culminate in rigid fanaticism that could destroy democratic processes if generalized throughout the community. . . . Only the doctrinaire would deprecate the moderate indifference that facilitates compromise." From Berelson, Lazarsfeld, and McPhee, "Democratic Practice and Political Theory," in *Political Elites in a Democracy*, ed. Peter Bachrach (New York: Atherton Press, 1971), p. 38. However, every past extension of citizen participation has also been opposed as likely to undermine good government.

[2] Michael Walzer, *Radical Principles* (New York: Basic Books, Inc., 1980), p. 134.

[3] Morgan Reynolds and Eugene Smolensky, *Public Expenditures, Taxes, and the Distribution of Income* (New York: Academic Press, 1977), pp. 91–96.

[4] This does not imply that inequalities are smaller under the economies that operated prior to free-enterprise economies. However, many economic development experts believe the first stages of economic modernization involve increased inequalities if relatively free markets dominate during those initial stages. See Samuel P. Huntington and Joan M. Nelson, *No Easy Choice* (Cambridge, MA: Harvard University Press, 1976), p. 75.

[5] Robert Moss, *The Collapse of Democracy* (London: Temple Smith, 1975), p. 48.

[6]Ibid., p. 55.

[7]In the United States in 1982–1983, average annual pre-tax income \
for the lowest-income 20 percent of all urban consumer units, but wa
(12.75 times higher) for the highest-income 20 percent, accordin
Statistical Abstract: 1986, p. 443. In 1984, the 26 percent of U.S. h
with the lowest incomes owned 10 percent of total household net worth, ...ereas
the 12 percent of households with the highest incomes owned 38 percent of total
household net worth. Thus, the wealthiest group had 8.2 times as great an
average household net worth as the poorest one. U.S. Department of Commerce,
Bureau of the Census, *Household Wealth and Asset Ownership: 1984* (Washington, D.C.: Current Population Reports, P-70, No. 7, July 1986), p. 2.

[8]This discussion is based largely on Douglas Rae, *Equalities* (Cambridge, MA:
Harvard University Press, 1981). It also draws upon R. H. Tawney, *Equality*
(London: Unwin Books, 1952).

[9]Rae, *Equalities*, p. 5.

[10]An example of compensatory inequality is any affirmative action program that
gives preferred access to jobs to minority-group members rather than majority
group members. However, such programs involve marginal equalization of
employment opportunities, not total equalization.

[11]"Amendments to the Constitution," in Alexander Hamilton, John Jay, and James
Madison, *The Federalist: A Commentary on the Constitution of the United States*
(New York: The Modern Library), pp. 598–99.

[12]National Conference of Catholic Bishops, *Second Draft: Pastoral Letter on
Catholic Social Teaching and the U.S. Economy* (Washington, D.C.: National
Conference of Catholic Bishops, 7 October 1985), p. 25.

[13]A notable example of this is the work of Amnesty International, which received a
Nobel Peace Prize for its efforts in 1977.

[14]Arend Lijphart presents the most comprehensive analysis of these two prototypes
in *Democracies: Patterns of Majoritarian and Consensus Government in Twenty-
One Countries* (New Haven: Yale University Press, 1984). This essay draws
heavily upon that book and three others: Arend Lijphart, *Democracy in Plural
Societies: A Comparative Exploration* (New Haven: Yale University Press, 1977);
Robert A. Dahl, *Polyarchy* (New Haven: Yale University Press, 1971); and G.
Bingham Powell, Jr., *Contemporary Democracies: Participation, Stability, and
Violence* (Cambridge, MA: Harvard University Press, 1982).

[15]Lijphart, *Democracies*, p. 4.

[16]W. Arthur Lewis, *Politics in West Africa* (London: George Allen and Unwin,
1965), pp. 64–65.

[17]Dahl, *Polyarchy*, p. 105.

[18]These four points are quoted from Lijphart, *Democracies*, p. 129.

[19]Lijphart, *Democracies*, pp. 127–35.

[20]Dahl, *Polyarchy*, p. 106.

[21]Ibid., p. 108.

[22]Conceiving of different levels of political controversy and action is not a new idea.
Political theorists since John Locke have differentiated between the normal level
and the constitutional level. Contemporary examples of this distinction are found
in (among others) John Rawls, *A Theory of Justice* (Cambridge, MA: Harvard
University Press, 1971); James M. Buchanan and Gordon Tullock, *The Calculus
of Consent* (Ann Arbor: University of Michigan Press, 1962); and Anthony

Downs, *Inside Bureaucracy* (Boston: Little, Brown & Company, 1967), chapter XIV.

[23]Bruce D. Berkowitz, *Stability in Political Systems: The Decision to Be Governed* (Unpublished, undated mimeographed manuscript).

[24]Lijphart, *Democracies*, p. 143.

[25]Ibid., p. 146.

[26]The term "nonrational" does not mean *irrational*; it has no pejorative connotation. Rather, as used here, it refers to motivations derived from goals that are not themselves rationally derivable from the broad human ends that most social scientists regard as universal, such as needs for food, shelter, and personal security.

[27]This concept was developed by Seymour Martin Lipset in *Political Man: The Social Basis of Politics* (Baltimore: Johns Hopkins University Press, 1981).

[28]Ibid., p. 77.

[29]Dahl, *Polyarchy*, pp. 115–18. Lebanon does not conform to this generalization— but then, Middle Eastern politics belie nearly all rational principles!

[30]Powell, *Contemporary Democracies*, p. 154.

[31]The *effective number of parties* is a measure that weighs the actual number of different political parties in a system by their relative electoral strength. Thus, a system with two parties that each get 50 percent of the vote has 2.0 effective parties. But if one party averages 70 percent of the vote, the effective number is 1.7. Lijphart calculated that the average effective number of parties in twenty-two democracies from 1945 to 1980 was highest in Finland (5.0) and lowest in the United States (1.9). See Lijphart, *Democracies*, pp. 116–23.

[32]These specific arrangements are described in Lijphart, *Democracies*, pp. 150–59.

[33]Only three of the twenty-two democracies studied by Lijphart had presidential systems: the United States, Finland, and the French Fifth Republic. Eighteen had parliaments in which the executive was dependent on the confidence of the legislature; one (Switzerland) had a parliament in which the executive was not dependent on the legislature's confidence, but it was a multiple executive. Thus, the parliamentary form is clearly dominant among existing democracies. See Lijphart, *Democracies*, p. 70.

[34]Ibid.

[35]The *effective number of parties* is defined in endnote 31.

[36]Lijphart, *Democracies*, p. 219.

[37]Lijphart, *Democracy in Plural Societies*, pp. 19–20. As proponents of this view, Lijphart cites M. G. Smith, Leonard Binder, Lucien W. Pye, and Samuel P. Huntington.

Name index

Arrow, K. 2

Berelson, B. 158
Bergson, A. 48
Berkowitz, B. 149
Berle, A.A. Jr 85
Binder, L. 160
Bingham Powell, G. Jr 152
Black, D. 59
Blau, P.M. 85
Buchanan, J.M. 159

Chiu, J.S.Y. 96
Clarke, E. 125
Colm, G. 48, 80, 81

Dahl, R. 145, 148, 151
Dahl, R.A. 2
Dalton, H. 1
Downs, A. 48, 159–60

Elbing, A.O. 96

Ferguson, M. 129
Fyfe, J. 125

Hotelling, H. 8, 9
Huntington, S.P. 158, 160

Lazarsfeld, P. 158
Lerner, A.P. 1
Lijphart, A. 142, 143, 146–9, 154–7,
    159, 160
Lindblom, C.E. 2
Lippmann, W. 60, 61
Lipset, S.M. 151, 160

Mannheim, K. 69
Maritain, J. 52
Marschak, J. 3
Marx, K. 148
McGuire, J.W. 96
McLuhan, M. 105
McNamara, R. 120
McPhee, W. 158
Means, G. 85
Merton, R.K. 19
Moss, R. 135

Nader, R. 109
Naisbitt, J. 129, 130
Nelson, J.M. 158

Peck, H.W. 1
Pye, L.W. 160

Rae, D. 136, 159
Rainwater, L. 123
Rawls, J. 159

Schubert, G. 58, 59, 65
Schumpeter, J.A. 2
Scott, W.R. 85
Smith, M.G. 160
Smithies, A. 8

Toffler, A. 129, 130
Truman, President 77
Tullock, G. 40–47, 91, 159

Walzer, M. 133
Wilde, O. 133
Williamson, O.E. 85, 90
Wilson, J.Q. 44